The Su~~~
Superpower
of Highly
Sensitive Person

Embrace Your Sensitivity and Thrive
in Your Relationships and Work

NORA HAYES

ISBN: 979-8-873-52293-4 (paperback)
ISBN: 979-8-873-52571-3 (hardcover)

First edition January 2024

Printed in the United States of America

TABLE OF CONTENTS

INTRODUCTION

I vividly remember the nervous butterflies in my stomach as I sat across from the career counselor. She peered at me through stylish glasses and asked plainly, "What do you want to be?" I stared back blankly, unsure how to respond.

You see, I've always been deeply moved by emotions. Sad films make me cry; beautiful music brings tears; I feel attuned to others' moods. I startle at small noises and get overwhelmed by bright lights, scratchy tags, and strong scents. I notice subtle details—the barista's twitching eyebrow, my friend's faint smile.

But such sensitivity carried a cost. I was teased for "overreacting" and learned to hide my tears. I struggled to fit in and often felt ashamed.

Sitting with that counselor, the familiar shame returned. She mistook my hesitation for confusion. But truly, I was still learning to embrace the essence of myself.

Through laughter, tears, connections, and hurts, I've found my way home. This book represents an invitation to your self-understanding. As Susan Cain wrote, "There is enough light for those who wish to see." I hope to gently illuminate your sensitivity as the gift it is.

What Does Sensitivity Mean?

"Highly sensitive person" often evokes images of crying easily or disliking noise and crowds. But it encompasses much more. At its core, high sensitivity means deeper mental processing and emotional responsiveness. You notice subtle textures, moods, and undercurrents in yourself, others, and life. Shades of gray dominate rather than black and white. Nuances captivate your senses, making life intensely meaningful.

While people link high sensitivity with avoiding sensory overload, it fundamentally signifies richer perception, reflection, and feeling. It is not an illness or flaw but an element of natural diversity—much like introversion and extraversion. Research shows sensitive types are creative, insightful, and attuned to emotional needs. By understanding your trait, you can harness its power while managing its intensity.

I aim to provide that understanding—so you can embrace your sensitivity as an invaluable gift. From examining what it means to exploring how to adapt, this book will guide you in nurturing self-compassion, relationships, and a gentle way of being that honors the depth within you.

However, temperament theory suggests that highly sensitive people run toward emotional nuance and meaning instead of running away from sensory stimulation. The richness you glean through experiences motivates you to continue soaking in life's poignancy.

Research by Dr. Elaine Aron, author of the groundbreaking book The Highly Sensitive Person, indicates that roughly 15-20% of people have an innate tendency toward high sensitivity. It's been observed across over 100 species—including fruit flies, dogs, cats, primates, and, of course, humans! This reveals high sensitivity isn't some abnormality or flaw but a naturally occurring trait supported by genetic biomarkers and distinct brain wiring.

What purpose does this heightened sensitivity serve?

For one, it promotes greater awareness of situational context so you can respond appropriately. You carefully observe people's facial expressions during conversations to discern their emotions and intentions. Your broad perspective, ability to think deeply, and attention to subtleties also spur creativity and problem-solving.

Plus, your insight supports caring for others—sensing their sadness, joy, insecurities, or needs.

However, living with sensory heightening comes with its curses and blessings. At times, your magnified sensitivity dials life's volume up to 11! Emotions flood your system. Your heart aches deeply in response to cruelty. Critical words sting like daggers; a pleasant touch feels glorious. Crowds, clutter, and chaos drain you. Beauty, inspiration, and kindness soothe and restore you.

Like most things, the paradox exists in harmony. Navigating both joy and overwhelm is part of the journey for HSPs. By learning to ride the waves, diverting from societal standards of "normal", and leaning into your true north, you get to witness life through a rich emotional lens—something from which the world tremendously benefits.

Why I Wrote This Book

In my journey of self-discovery as a highly sensitive person, the most helpful step was knowing I wasn't alone or "too" sensitive. Untold numbers of HSPs around the globe share similar traits and face comparable challenges. Witnessing inspirational HSPs thriving in their lives and careers motivated me to embrace my sensitivity confidently too.

However, if you're reading this, perhaps you still struggle with bouts of overwhelm or even shame around your sensitive nature. Maybe you haven't found the right strategies for navigating intense stimuli and emotions. Possibly, you grapple with conflicts and miscommunications frequently. Or you instinctively avoid leadership positions or careers involving high visibility or pressure.

My heartfelt wish is to guide you to a place of self-acceptance, compassion, insight, and empowerment. By understanding the latest scientific discoveries about high sensitivity, implementing practical coping strategies tailored to your nature, and awakening to your unique strengths, I hope that you'll embark upon your hero's journey with courage and wisdom.

The world desperately needs people like us—highly aware co-creators and vision-aries catching glimpses into the future through our emotionally attuned lens. Our collaboratively minded, insightful, empathic, and creative essence helps soothe a weary world. But first, we must boldly embrace ourselves.

What You Can Expect to Gain From This Book

Upon reading this book, you will come away understanding yourself pro-foundly—why you experience the world uniquely, how your brain is wired, and what motivates you intrinsically. The veil will lift, helping you recognize your greatest challenges along with your noteworthy superpowers.

You'll discover targeted techniques to prevent overwhelm and emotional flooding, plus simple self-care strategies to incorporate into daily routines. Additionally, key communication approaches will enhance all your relationships. Plus, you'll gain confidence and clarity to transform how you operate in work and social settings—without burning yourself out.

Alongside grounding practical strategies, inspirational quotes and real-life HSP stories dispel limiting beliefs and affirm that highly sensitive people can follow their heart's calling and boldly contribute their gifts. You'll witness fellow HSPs thriving in careers like counseling, the arts, advocacy, research, writing, and lead-ership in various sectors.

Most significantly, this book serves as an anchor during stormy seas and a torch shining light on your unfolding journey toward self-acceptance. You are perfect and complete, woefully imperfect, and everything in between. May you embrace the fullness of your sensitive soul. Now come, take my hand. Let's venture inward together, meet all that stirs there, whisper soothing words, and begin believing what we discover.

Navigating Life's Highways and Byways as a Highly Sensitive Person

Gentle wanderer of life's highways and byways, whether you picked up this book by fate or intuition, I am thrilled to have you traversing this path with me. As you embark on the journey of unearthing your exquisite sensitive self, we'll be your trusty guides in highlighting meaningful milestones, pausing to soak in expansive views, and supporting you when the road gets rocky. Consider me your trusted sherpa, committed to your self-development, empowerment, and joy.

This expedition invites you to soak in colours, textures, sounds, and vistas that perfectly suit your heightened aesthetic radar. By being sensitive-centric, focusing inward instead of how you "should" navigate society, you get to embrace all of your precious emotional spectrum boldly yet organically. Happiness, grief, anxiety, overwhelm, joy—they all have a special place on the vast canvas of YOU.

During overwhelming moments, picture me offering refreshing sips of lemon-infused water or fanning you gently. Or when you're coasting on inspiration's surge, I'll be dancing gleefully and marveling at your creative spirit taking flight! Whenever harsh headlights glare, making you wince, I'll draw the window shades. And when glorious sunbeams inspire you to soak in their blessing, I'll be basking joyfully beside you.

Through calm seas and stormy ones, by relatoring rest stops and triumphant mountain peaks, I am endlessly awed by your kaleidoscope nature. You possess a rare ability to soak in life's vibrant colours and subtle pastel undertones most miss or dismiss.

What a precious gift!

My deepest longing is that you feel safe to expand into YOU fully—knowing I'll be here still to cheer you onward, umbrellas or pom-poms in hand.

So breathe deeply as you absorb these words. Let them seep slowly into your essence, awakening you to the profound truth. You are a gentle warrior, set apart to infuse this world with the nuanced emotional wisdom it desperately requires. Our adventures lie ahead... Once you're ready, I'll gladly accompany you wherever you lead!

Come, let's dare boldly be who we are—together.

Onward!

CHAPTER 1

THE NATURE OF SENSITIVITY

"The soul is dyed the color of its thoughts. Think only on those things that are in line with your principles and can bear the light of day." - Marcus Aurelius

How profoundly that ancient wisdom resonates today in our journey of unraveling the intricate facets of sensitivity. As we open the doorway to Chapter 1 and cross the threshold into The Nature of Sensitivity, I invite you to lean in and soak up insights illuminating your inner world. Leave biases or judgments behind and open your mind to new perspectives that affirm your authentic self.

In The Tapestry of Traits section, we'll trace the flowing threads that interweave to form the unique fabric of highly sensitive people. I'll share how I came to grasp the inherent value in attributes I once deemed "flaws" - like my tearfulness during poignant moments or acute awareness of injustice and discord. Together, we'll reflect on times when you may have felt "too much" and explore how sensation, perception, emotional responsiveness, and empathy color your inner seas.

Next, as we traverse The Science of Sensitivity, fascinating research will affirm heightened sensitivity as an innate trait tied to genetics, brain structure, and nervous system functioning. Did theories around "fight or flight" never quite resonate for you? We'll discuss the highly responsive SPS—sensory processing sensitivity—and why some process stimuli deeply.

Finally, in A Nuanced Nervous System, the concept of "miswiring" gets redefined. You'll gain clarity around overwhelm triggers and start implementing tailored techniques to ride sensory and emotional waves. Ultimately, science validates sensitive qualities as differences, not deficiencies. Through understanding your hardwiring, you write a new story of self-trust.

Come, take my hand as we continue. Revelations await!

a. What is High Sensitivity: Characteristics and Traits

High sensitivity simply indicates deeper mental processing and emotional reactivity. HSPs notice more about their environment, think deeply before reacting, and feel emotions intensely. Their sensitive nervous system essentially functions like a highly perceptive microscope and telescope, constantly tuning into subtleties within themselves, others, and their surroundings that elude most people.

Key traits and characteristics

Elaine Aron's D.O.E.S. acronym summarizes key high sensitivity characteristics:

Depth of Processing – HSPs naturally process more deeply, thoroughly, and slowly. You carefully observe others' nonverbal expressions during conversations to discern their feelings and intentions. Before responding, you ponder ideas extensively.

Overarousal – You rapidly become overwhelmed by emotional or sensory stimuli. Loud noises startle you. You cry easily watching poignant movies. Criticism cuts especially deep. However, you relish life's exquisite beauty and simple pleasures too.

Emotional Reactivity and Empathy – HSPs experience all feelings profoundly—happiness, sadness, grief, and joy. You immediately sense others' moods and can literally feel their emotions. This emotional mirroring helps foster compassion.

Sensory Sensitivity – You detect subtle sensory details most individuals overlook, whether someone's fleeting frown or softly ticking clock. However, intense stimuli like glaring light easily frazzle you. Your nervous system processes everything more thoroughly, for better or worse.

Innate Temperament

Extensive research conducted worldwide shows that sensory processing sensitivity represents an innate temperament type occurring across 100 species. As an HSP, you were likely born sensitive versus solely shaped by your environment.

In fact, genetics underpin about 50% of the SPS trait. This means high sensitivity runs in families and can't be altered. You can, however, change your perspective on sensitivity as an advantageous gift instead of a hindrance.

Potent Powers

Transforming how you view high sensitivity proves pivotal. Once embraced as an innate difference and asset, your potent powers shine. Consider what evolutionary benefits increased sensitivity offers society:

- Enhanced threat detection
- Cautious decision-making
- Heightened conscience/adherence to rules
- Exceptional creativity
- Artistic and inventive vision
- Rich, intuitive wisdom
- Innate understanding of others' feelings
- Profound capacity to heal and empathize

The next time someone jokingly calls you "too sensitive," recognize they simply lack the capacity to perceive what you do. Then, compassionately educate them on the exquisite wonder of your rare perspective.

For now, my eyes twinkle like the enchanting lights of childhood when beholding life's radiant beauty. I embrace my high sensitivity as the magical blessing it truly is. Eyes wide, I courageously invite you to soak in each glorious, poignant detail too. Our gift is meant to be shared.

b.   The Science Behind High Sensitivity: Exploring the Research

I'll never forget the goosebumps that prickled my arms as I first learned about Elaine Aron's revolutionary research on highly sensitive people (HSPs) during my undergraduate psychology course. As my professor described measurable differences in the nervous systems and genetics of HSPs, I hung onto her every word. It was as if brilliant scientists had peered directly into my biology, seen past my skin into the very essence of ME, and declared, "Aha! Here's why you are the way you are!"

For the first time in my life, I felt truly seen and understood. My nervous system wasn't as defective as I had presumed. Rather, subtle genetic variations produced my enhanced sensitivity, emotional responsiveness, and rich inner life. This innate temperament also occurred naturally in 15-20% of the population.

As my professor elaborated on additional studies, I excitedly scribbled down titles and authors, eager to devour every scientific morsel, validating my long-misunderstood trait. I left class that evening tired yet wired from the adrenaline of new discovery. Upon realizing I wasn't alone, I sensed my burgeoning self-acceptance taking root and blossoming that day. Countless others shared this remarkable sensitivity gift. The factual seeds planted through ingenious research liberated me to finally embrace the exquisite orchid I was meant to be.

The Sensitive Nervous System

While the causes of sensory processing sensitivity (SPS) remain unclear, research suggests pronounced differences in the nervous systems of HSPs. Our sensory systems essentially possess more receptive antennae able to detect subtle cues. We also have more responsive brake pedals primed to pause and evaluate potential threats. This combo produces enhanced awareness of our surroundings and inner worlds alike.

For instance, brain scans show HSPs have increased activity in regions related to attention, action planning, and decision-making. Additional blood flow likely feeds hungry neurons processing information more thoroughly. Visual or auditory data streams at turbo speed to highly active tracking centers. You might call our nervous system a Formula One race car while less sensitive individuals putter along in Toyotas!

The amygdala also flashes boldly on our brain scans. Since this region governs emotional processing and arousal regulation, it explains why we feel things so profoundly. Our easily flooded systems broadcast strong "e-motion" signals, creating ready-for-action cellular pathways. Suddenly, the intensity of our outsized reactions makes perfect sense! Blame it on a buzzing beehive of neurons and hormones.

It's not that our sensitive systems are innately flawed; rather, they are specialized equipment designed to detect threats AND glory in life's beauty. We don't merely hear a song; we feel its melody reverberating through our soul. Our nervous systems don't simply operate on overdrive. They are Lamborghinis built for emotionally resonant journeys.

The Genetic Factor

While environmental factors contribute, researchers confirm genetics underlie nearly 50% of high sensitivity. Specific gene variants shape our sensory receptivity, evidencing this as an inborn trait. Population studies also show sensitivity running strongly in families—further suggesting heightened sensitivity gets passed on to future generations.

Recent human genome analyses pinpoint gene differences related to serotonin activity, arousal regulation, and empathy as common in HSPs. Such gene variations clearly alter nervous system development, emotional reactions, and social behavior too. It's fascinating how a simple divergence in DNA script can so profoundly influence the way we navigate life!

Now, researchers are investigating exactly how such genetic divergence activates downstream effects biologically and psychologically. Studies already indicate more vulnerability to anxiety, overstimulation, and burnout in HSPs. Just think if scientists uncovered specific gene therapies to help sensitive people better regulate emotions or recover from stress!

For now, simply realizing our genetic uniqueness holds substantial power. We can finally forgive ourselves for feeling things "too deeply" or struggling to filter stimuli. High sensitivity is not some personal failing or flaw. Nor do we need to keep striving to "strengthen" our sensitive system somehow. We must only embrace our exquisite neurological wiring and then adapt environments to empower our inborn potential. For in the right supportive habitat, an orchid will thrive as nature intended!

c. Understanding Sensory Processing Sensitivity

The Intricacies of Sensory Processing Sensitivity

Sensory Processing Sensitivity (SPS) refers to having a highly sensitive nervous system that meticulously processes subtleties in the environment. As we dive deeper into the science behind this trait, it's crucial to first distinguish SPS from the medical condition Sensory Processing Disorder.

While both involve sensory sensitivity, they have distinct mechanisms. Sensory Processing Disorder is a condition where the brain struggles to modulate sensory input, leading to challenges in daily life functioning. On the other hand, SPS is an innate trait where the nervous system is extra responsive to positive and negative stimuli. This leads to greater emotional and cognitive processing that can be a strength, not just a hindrance.

The Highly Sensitive Nervous System in Action

Research shows the sensitive nervous system reacts more strongly in response to sensations and situations. We see this through the easily activated "fight or flight" stress response that can be set off by events most people find unremarkable.

Calming down also tends to take longer in highly sensitive people—their "rest and digest" nervous system is slower to kick in. This leaves some in a constant state of tension, vulnerable to quicker burnout. Understanding this mechanism helps guide effective regulation techniques.

Capturing the Sensitivity Story Inside the Brain

Cutting-edge brain imaging techniques are unlocking the neural hallmarks of sensitivity. fMRI scans demonstrate highly sensitive people exhibit amplified activity in brain regions tied to awareness, sensory integration, empathy, and even vision processing. Parts like the anterior cingulate cortex and amygdala fire up more readily, attuning HSPs to environmental subtleties, including others' mood shifts.

These studies also detect connectivity differences in areas governing emotional processing and regulation. The unique wiring patterns clarify why strong sensations can flood sensitive systems. Yet, as intense as the reactions may be, optimal brain health hinges on embracing your whole neurobiology.

Ongoing Revelations Through Sensitivity Research

Exciting studies continue surfacing that further validate the sensory processing sensitivity trait. From genetic links to physiological biomarkers and behavioral observations, science consistently demonstrates this as a hardwired, naturally occurring temperament.

And, while heightened sensitivity introduces distinct challenges, research reminds us of the remarkable gifts too—exceptional perceptiveness, creativity, intuition, and empathy. Studies empower us to dispel limiting beliefs and make sensitive-centric changes by illuminating sensitivity's evolutionary roots and real-life impact.

A Snapshot of the Highly Sensitive Brain

While much about sensitivity's intricacies remain unknown, preliminary brain imaging captured captivating insights. One study found highly sensitive people exhibit more brain activity in response to others' emotions—especially positive ones from close loved ones. The active circuitry suggests an inherent talent for self-other integration and empathy.

Another functional MRI experiment detected amplified visual and attention region engagement among HSPs. This backs existing behavioral research indicating more elaborate processing of sensory stimuli. Both studies position sensitive nervous systems as specialized instruments that enrich and expand life's experience.

The Balancing Act of Living Sensitively

Embarking on the journey of embracing your one-of-a-kind sensitive nervous system can feel adventurous yet daunting. We become gracefully attuned human instruments by learning to ride the waves between glorious and overwhelming. Soon, you'll be soaking in each subtle sensory delight and riding inspiration's surges shamelessly. But for now, let's continue venturing inward together, one compassionate step at a time.

Conclusion

As we conclude uncovering key facets of sensitivity, I'm struck by how much still lies ahead on our collective adventure. Perhaps you feel similarly—awed by science's endorsements yet eager for practical ways to thrive. If so, journey with me into the next phase of demystifying what sensitivity means for our daily lives and relationships.

This vital knowledge awaits!

CHAPTER 2

RECOGNIZING HIGH SENSITIVITY

I'll never forget the tightness in my chest during that fateful session with my therapist. We'd explored my sensitivity for weeks, turning over glimmering insights about my unique perceptual gifts like sea glass shimmering in the sand. But as she gazed at me with probing yet kind eyes and asked bluntly, "What core beliefs might you carry about being too emotional or reactive?" I froze. Though we'd built trust discussing my sensory overwhelm, shame still swelled discussing weaknesses. I stared at the sage green walls, wishing I could melt into its calming hue and camouflage my flush of unease.

As the stillness thickened between us, I sensed her compassion and let vulnerability unfurl. "I'm afraid if I fully embrace my emotional intensity instead of hiding it, I'll lose relationships," I whispered hesitantly. Thus began my journey of recognizing sensitivity's blessing while unlearning the curse I'd presumed it to be.

In Identifying If You Are Highly Sensitive, questions dismantling limiting mindsets helped me view emotional receptivity as an innate gift instead of a hindrance. No longer labeling my tearfulness a deficiency, I began scripting a self-honoring narrative about my distinctive perceptual talents that transformed how I walk through life.

Just as a caterpillar relinquishes the confines of its cocoon to emerge resplendent, recognizing high sensitivity necessitates shedding old perspectives about yourself. Here, clarity takes shape, delineating unique sensitivity characteristics versus overlapping ones with introversion or anxiety. And tapping into creativity's flowing stream once shame dissolves, I sensed more ideas surfacing.

First, spend time in the mirror, beholding the original being gazing back. The most crucial metamorphosis unfolds within.

a. Self-Discovery: Identifying if You Are Highly Sensitive

Sitting across from my therapist, vulnerability swelled within as she gently asked if I hid emotional intensity to maintain relationships. This marked the start of my self-discovery, assessing my sensitivity with radical self-honesty. Through questions exposing limiting beliefs and nurturing new perspectives, I gained clarity. Was my tearfulness a deficiency or gift? Her guidance helped me view sensitivity as an innate talent instead of a hindrance, transforming my self-narrative.

We explored my childhood imaginary worlds, realizing they were early evidence of sensitivity, not weirdness. Overstimulation overwhelmed me, yet creativity flowed when alone. My therapist suggested my perceptive nervous system resembles a finely tuned instrument—I pick up on subtleties others miss. This resonance explains why emotions feel like storms rather than information. I learned observing their ebb and flow with mindfulness, not judgment, allows wisdom to emerge.

As my journal memories surfaced, I recognized my emotional radar accurately detecting truth or falseness in situations, like swiftly sensing an arrogant date's facade or being compelled to stand up for underdogs. I acknowledged my rich inner world as a wellspring for creativity, not something to hide. Understanding high sensitivity as difference, not deficiency, illuminated natural gifts I'd dismissed—perceptiveness, emotional attunement, imagination. Finally, embracing my full radiance rippled out and allowed me to forge deeper connections and follow my intuition.

Exploring Your Sensitivity Experience

Do memories of vivid imaginary worlds confirm you're highly sensitive? Did chaotic playgrounds distress you as a child while alone time brought peace? Realizing these early coping strategies often indicate emotional receptivity freed me from shame. Suspecting your extra sensitivity explains why being called shy or withdrawn in childhood also resonates.

Consider which senses feel uncomfortably amplified—maybe noise and scents overwhelm you. Do crowds drain you? What subtle shifts in art or nature enthrall you? Spend time reflecting: when has emotional perceptiveness guided your intuition accurately? Do you tear up easily watching poignant films?

My therapist's questions revealed sensitivity's blessings that once felt like curses. These gentle inquiries highlighted my natural gifts while nurturing self-compassion. Exploring your experiences similarly allows wisdom to emerge. Be patient, recording insights in a journal. Recognizing high sensitivity traits is the doorway to embracing their beauty. You were born sensitive for a reason: to pick up on what others miss, transform environments with your emotional radar, and follow creative passions unfettered by limitation. Suffocating sensitivity's sparkle dims your light and this world's. Realizing high sensitivity catalyzes transforming how you move through life and life itself as your talents touch others.

Highly Sensitive Person Self-Assessments

Elaine Aron and Arthur Aron, in 1997, developed the Highly Sensitive Person Scale featuring these questions accessing sensory processing sensitivity. Consider your reactions: which resonate? Do light and sound overwhelm you? Do emotional nuances in films deeply move you? Does competing under observation make you nervous? Online self-assessments utilizing similar prompts also estimate your sensitivity location on the continuum.

Tuning into my responses, I understood why excessive stimuli bother me and quiet solo time feels restorative. Assessing what overtaxes your system provides clarity on where establishing boundaries is wise. There's no absolute cutoff deter-mining high sensitivity. But candidly investigating traits and questioning if they enhance or limit you uncovers your experience's contours. Additional self-reflection tools can also pinpoint subdued childhood wounding that skewed negative perceptions about emotional intensity.

Be patient and non-judgmental, recording insights over time. What initially seemed jarring often transforms understanding sensitivity's nature, letting it empower rather than trap you. Unlearning assumptions is a metamorphosis—the caterpillar doesn't recognize its beauty as it relinquishes limiting ideations within the cocoon. Your emerging wings will feel lighter flying with truth. These questions are doorways illuminating your gorgeous wholeness awaiting awareness. You were born sensitive, perceptive, emotionally wise, and with creative talents because the world uniquely needs your abilities. It's time to let them shine bright.

b. Differentiating Sensitivity from Introversion, Shyness, and Anxiety

My therapist gently asked if hiding my emotions maintained relationships. This marked my self-discovery, assessing sensitivity with honesty. Her questions birthed new perspectives about my gifts versus hindrances. Was emotional intensity a deficiency or talent? Our talks shifted my views—sensitivity became an innate ability, not an obstacle, changing my self-narrative.

We explored childhood imaginary worlds, realizing they indicated early sensitivity evidence, not weirdness. Playground chaos overwhelmed while alone time brought peace and creativity. She explained my perceptive nervous system resembles a finely tuned instrument, noticing subtleties others miss. This resonance clarified why emotions feel like storms, not information. I learned observing their ebb and flow with mindfulness, not judgment, allows wisdom.

My memories confirmed that my emotional radar accurately detects truth or falseness in situations, like sensing an arrogant date's facade or standing up for underdogs. I acknowledged my rich inner world's wellspring creativity, not something to hide. Recognizing sensitivity's difference, not deficiency, illuminated natural gifts I'd dismissed: perceptiveness, emotional attunement, imagination. Finally embracing my radiance lets it empower connections and intuition.

An extroverted highly sensitive person has a great need for constant contact yet also protects from overstimulation—opposing forces. Outwardly warm and expressive with a small circle of loyal friends, they dislike small talk, absorbing group tensions quickly. Leadership roles happen through conviction, not preference. They think before acting, they need novelty and meaning, not status. My gifts differ from pure introversion. I gain energy from alone time yet wither without inspired action. We share emotional depth but relate to stimulation uniquely.

Sensory Sensitivity and Shyness

Was I born shy or taught fear of judgment? No one enters life shy. Yet sensitive children may seem so, carefully observing before socializing, fearful of new energies. Past overwhelm teaches avoiding new people not worth exhausting interactions. We know scrutiny hurts deeply, so built-in lie detectors compel hiding, worried about being "found out" to be different. Trauma and criticism warp perspectives about emotional intensity. Healing requires recognizing that the fear of ridicule stems from absorbing negativity too intensely. Then sensitivity's poetry lets it empower rather than trap you.

I mistook childhood fussiness and imaginary friends for shyness when, actually, emotional overload necessitated escape. My therapist helped me understand desiring yet dreading human closeness signaled high sensitivity, not social anxiety. She explained sensory processing sensitivity means stimulated more intensely, so shy people pleasers like me require downtime to process life's constant input. Life still overwhelms me at times, but awareness of this trait transformed my self-compassion. I create space protecting my nervous system and boundaries from people-pleasing. Understanding the highly sensitive person explained my observed shyness, freeing me to embrace confidence.

Parsing Anxiety From Sensitivity

Did playing childhood percussion rouse anxiety or sensitivity? Loud noise created acute discomfort; my heart racing, breathing shallow. I longed to escape the stimulating assembly. Anxious or sensory overload? Discerning the difference still challenges me. I cry easily watching poignant films. Do sorrowful stories elicit anxiety or emotional attunement? My environment impacts everything. Food, scents, and fabrics annoyingly amplify sometimes. Is irritation anxiety or sensory processing sensitivity?

I asked my therapist about this constantly. She explained anxiety disorders incorporate fearing harmless things. Sensitivity means your perceptual nervous system processes information deeply—joy and suffering. My angst typically links directly to overstimulation. We parsed reasons for my panic attacks. Fear of judgment, toxic past? Or noisy crowds plus hunger? Trauma breeds anxiety. But outside conditions also overtax sensitive systems. Figuring out your emotional ABCs means dividing anxiety provoked by stressors versus overly intense environmental responses.

Highly sensitive people live with more anxiety than others, she says. Healing my traumas and practicing self-care changed everything. When situations trigger discomfort, I consciously check: is this anxiety or sensitivity overload? If sensitivity, I retreat for calm rather than spiraling about anxiety. Sometimes, both intertwine, so I utilize coping strategies accordingly. I still unravel life's turbulence with extra mindfulness. But compassion for my perceptive wiring settled my once frenzied thoughts. My sensory processing sensitivity will never depart, but better boundaries, emotional awareness, and self-nurturing transformed my perspective. Dwelling in this skin, life feels less loud and more balanced.

c. The Positive Aspects of High Sensitivity

Seeing the Bright Side: The Positive Aspects of High Sensitivity

I used to only see the downsides of my high sensitivity—the overwhelm, the intensity, the self-consciousness. But with time and self-understanding, I've come to appreciate and even treasure many positive aspects too. My sensitivity brings painful challenges but also beautiful gifts. Let's shine a light on some major upsides.

Experiencing Life's Depth and Richness

As an HSP, I don't just skim life's surface; I plunge right into its depths, textures, colors, and feelings. Like sinking slowly into a warm bath, I let myself steep in experiences. Concerts captivate me so much I get chills. Nature's beauty moves me to tears. Acts of human kindness make my heart swell. The world feels profoundly meaningful. This intensity is a double-edged sword, for sure. But I also get to live life in Technicolor while others watch in black and white.

Empathy, Intuition and Emotional Insight

I often know how people are feeling even before they speak. I read moods and energy like words on a page. Sometimes, I sense coming conflict before anyone else. This emotional intuition guides me in relationships and shows me how to support loved ones. I also have deep wells of empathy. Suffering sends shockwaves through me, compelling me to help. Being so attuned to sadness means I better understand life's hurts. My sensitivity makes me intensely human.

Noticing Life's Hidden Beauty

While others rush by, I linger to appreciate life's quiet details—the way dawn softly lights the sky, how rain patterns a window, dappled sunshine through trees. My senses drink in texture, color, and sound so palpably. I find beauty everywhere because I look deeper and longer with the eyes of my imagination. This magical perception makes the world feel richer.

Creativity and Self-Expression

I suspect most great artists and innovators leaned sensitive. When you perceive the world vividly, translating those sensations into expression feels natural. My journals overflow with reflections, dreams, memories. Creating brings me joy. And since sensitivity means picking up on nuances others miss, I offer a unique lens on life through my art. The world certainly doesn't lack perspectives resembling everyone else's. Mine add fresh angles.

Forming Deep Connections

I don't open up easily or have a wide social circle. But once someone has earned my trust, our bond runs bone-deep. I give relationship my all—understanding, acceptance, active listening. I make people feel truly seen. And I only let in those offering reciprocity. My few intimates appreciate this loyalty. Not spreading myself thin lets me nurture profound ties. Depth over breadth in friendship suits me fine.

Practicing Radical Self-Care

No one can withstand overload's storms without good self-care. And since I get overwhelmed easily, I've become an expert in preventively nourishing myself. I carve out alone time, quiet spaces, and intentional solitude. Making my needs non-negotiable boundaries keeps me balanced. And I surround myself with safe people so I don't constantly ward off emotional danger. Honoring my sensitivity this way lets me thrive.

As you can see, while heightened sensitivity poses trials requiring fortitude, it also unlocks life's magic. We perceive what others miss, transform pain into art, nurture deep bonds, and drink from beauty's chalice. Our gifts uplift this world. But first, we must honor them within ourselves.

d. The relationship between sensitivity and empathy, creativity, and intuition

My heightened sensitivity shows up in many ways—getting overwhelmed in crowds, moved to tears by poignant songs, noticing subtle energies in a room. But it also connects deeply to other key parts of who I am—my empathy, creativity, and intuition. Let's explore these profound ties.

Me, An Empath? The Blurry Lines Between Sensitivity and Empathy

I used to think "empath" sounded almost paranormal, like psychics who can read minds or emotions. But it turns out many highly sensitive people are also empaths. We don't have magical powers, but we feel things deeply, sometimes even absorbing others' emotions. I didn't realize how much I took on people's feelings until I became overwhelmed by unfamiliar moods. Learning to set empathic boundaries helped me distinguish someone else's sadness from my own. Now, I know my sensitivity and empathy go hand-in-hand.

Creativity Rising: How Sensitivity Sparks the Imagination

Since childhood, vivid imaginary worlds unfurled inside me. And I turned those inner visions into stories, poems, and paintings. However, I assumed making art was just a hobby until a therapist suggested my creativity was related to my finely tuned nervous system. When you perceive subtleties and textures others miss, it spills out in creative expression. She was right; channeling my sensitivity into art feels healing, almost involuntary. Now, I see it as a gift, not a distraction. My creativity helps me translate life's complex emotions through metaphors and symbols. It's insight and clarity captured in images—sensitivity made visible.

Intuition as Inner Compass: Learning to Trust My Gut

As an HSP, I often know things without quite knowing how I know, like sensing when people hide feelings behind smiles or when a situation isn't what it appears. For years, I doubted and silenced this inner voice. But it almost always proved accurate, an emotional radar-detecting truth. So, I'm learning to trust my intuition—deep wisdom channeled through my sensitive nervous system. Now, first reactions guide me; that "no" feeling warns me away from bad choices. While logic still has merit, I tune in first to intuitive whispers. They haven't steered me wrong yet. And paired with empathy, intuition is my most soulful guide.

So now, I see how interwoven sensitivity's gifts are—emotional insight, creative expression, inner guidance. Together, they make up the tapestry of my rich experience. Sensitivity lets me inhabit life so fully, feeling, perceiving, and under-standing its nature. What once seemed like a heavy burden is actually a profound connection.

Conclusion

As we've explored, sensitivity brings both painful struggles and profound bless-ings. While easily overwhelmed and intensely reactive, we also passionately engage in life's depths. Our emotional attunement nurtures empathy yet overflows, at times, into anxiety. But the same receptivity also unlocks creativity, intuition, and meaning.

Seeing sensitivity's poetry lets us transform limiting beliefs into self-compassion. We relinquish notions of weakness to embrace natural talents serving a higher pur-pose. For in truth, the gifts of sensitivity uplift our world but first require honor within ourselves.

Yet, balancing intense perception with equanimity remains an ever-unfolding jour-ney. As life presents new seasons, we must actively nourish resilience to weather sensitivity's storms. Introducing self-care early prevents crises later.

In the next chapter, we'll explore useful strategies for navigating common sen-sitivity-related pitfalls. Discover how to short-circuit destructive shame spirals, establish healthy boundaries, communicate needs effectively, and more. Healing misperceptions transforms sensitivity from curse to blessing.

We'll also discuss reducing stimulation through environmental adjustments, find-ing safe social niches, and developing anxiety-coping tools. Use wisdom gathered from fellow sensitive sojourners further down the path, for community sustains when loneliness arises.

I invite you to approach the upcoming topics with compassion for the gloriously complex beings we are. Our distinctive way of inhabiting life is not broken but beautifully, remarkably whole. We need never again to minimize our sensitivity but rather empower it with self-knowledge. Are you ready to truly thrive?

The journey continues...

CHAPTER 3

NAVIGATING CHALLENGES

The crashing waves beckoned, promising adventure and refreshment on that sweltering summer day. As a child, I relished plunging into the ocean's cool blue depths, savoring the caress of salty breezes. Yet amidst towering waves, I once felt an unexpected panic rise like bile, nearly drowning under relentless walls of water. Choking back fear as Dad scooped up my flailing body, I realized a force, both wondrous and treacherous, dwelled beneath the sea's calm surface.

Like the ocean, sensitivity also cycles between poetic splendor and overwhelming tumult. Glorious tranquility assuredly competes with unexpected storms in an HSP's perceived inner seas. One moment, life's stimulation delights like dolphins dancing through gleaming crests, souls soaked in beauty. The next, all sensory input assaults like sharks in a feeding frenzy, threatening to capsize my equilibrium utterly.

While harnessing sensitivity's magic, we must acknowledge its formidable storms too. Gathering fellow sojourners' wisdom, we discover tools protecting our essence when walls of water arrive, for with compassion and self-knowledge, we ride life's tides, preserving exquisite perceptual gifts uniquely calibrating our distinctive essence.

Shall we dive deeper, exploring useful coping strategies that transform curses into blessings when sensitivity's storms inevitably arise?

The currents call, and new insights await!

a. Challenges of Being Highly Sensitive (the unique experiences HSPs have in different environments)

My sensitivity opens doors to life's poetry, but storms arise too. While reveling gifts in the last chapter, we must also map storms awaiting sensitive voyagers. Today's trek reveals useful strategies for meeting sensitivity's trials so we ride waves without drowning. Gathering collective wisdom from fellow travelers, we discover tools protecting our distinctive essence. Prepare for tempestuous seas, but take heart; with self-knowledge, we can thrive. Onward to the swirling currents...

Overstimulation: My Brain on Overdrive

Like a high-performance car, my sensitive nervous system requires premium fuel and care. But revving full throttle nonstop inevitably causes collapse. Daily, I absorb hundreds more sensory details than others—that input overflows limited containers. So, quiet downtime lets overflow drain, so I restart refreshed, not burnt out.

Without stillness, even minor irritants like fluorescent lights, scratchy shirts, or loud laughter may spark overwhelm. My perceptual nervous system no longer filters input, just floods. Soon, emotional storms drench relationships, and physical symptoms manifest like headaches or exhaustion. I blame circumstances, not realizing overstimulation saturates me. Establishing healthy boundaries and self-care practices prevents such common HSP pitfalls.

Sensory Overload and its Impact

Once flooded, I'm captive to sensitivity's storms, unable to escape pounding rains. Scents assault nostrils, sunlight stabs eyeballs, each shirt tag razor sharp. My haven becomes a hellish prison. Social plans canceled, I hibernate in dark, quiet rooms, hoping to recover equilibrium.

But isolation further stresses relationships. Friends and family cannot fathom such extreme reactions to seemingly normal environments. They demand I "push through" discomfort without comprehending my nervous system lacks such resilience. But just as muscles require rest between intense workouts, sensitive systems also need repose to rebuild strength. Pushing collapse helps none; nurture restores all.

Overthinking

My multifaceted mind also curses and blesses. Gifted creating kaleidoscopic inner universes, imagination tantalizes yet also taunts. I replay past mistakes on endless loops, ruminating over better choices. Or future worries commandeer sleep as I script catastrophe. Always churning options, my hamster wheel thoughts exhaust, yet it cannot rest. Without stillness, thoughts themselves bombard and overwhelm. I yearn to escape the labyrinthian mind looping fear, regret, judgment. Yet overthinking often spotlights areas for growth too, does it not, my friends? Life's complexity requires deep processing, not shallow skimming. So, I learn to balance reflection and action.

Managing Criticism

Further intensifying emotional storms, criticism cuts deepest, triggering past wounds. Since childhood, people called me "too sensitive," so I built thick skins, or so I thought. Yet sharp words still slip through armor, eviscerating heart and self-worth. I replay critiques for years, layering additional self-judgment upon original pain. Desperate to halt escalating shame spirals before they crush vibrancy, I create new inner allies. These champions remind me no person defines my essence. When storms arise, I weather first turbulence supported by self-compassion.

Time Pressure

I also loathe rushed schedules, upending my precarious equilibrium. My sensitive nervous system requires meticulous planning before engaging external demands. Sudden appointments or hurried deadlines spur panic, not productivity. Lacking dead space on calendars guarantees stress reactions sabotaging health. People accuse me of laziness or procrastination when really overscheduling gives no room for preparation. Without nurturing my introverted tendency to withdraw and deeply contemplate the challenges ahead, I cannot succeed. Please understand fast-paced modern life clashes with ancient rhythms my body requires. Have patience; you'll reap rich rewards.

Addiction

To numb sensitivity's storms, I sometimes soothed frayed nerves with dangerous elixirs promising peace. Society celebrates alcohol, dulling life's too-muchness. So long, I believed drinking's temporary magic outweighed consequences like depression or relationships eroding. But just as rivers carved the Grand Canyon's magnificent gorge, so too did addiction insidiously etch pain's grooves within. No longer do I trade wholeness for fleeting relief. Healthier boundaries and self-care practices grant the tranquility substances falsely advertised. I face storms now boldly sober, a choice I am proud of.

Inner Critic

I also battle relentless inner critics distorting self-perception. Their sly whispers echo old wounds: "You don't belong here. Just give up, failure." As a besieged city believes enemies at the gate herald apocalypse, so too do I pronounce myself an irredeemable failure based on single struggles. But embodied life necessitates missteps on the winding path to joy. So I build kinder inner allies, reminding me that I traverse this journey beautifully, even exquisitely flawed. Your company also nourishes. Together, we move gently through madness toward wholeness.

Alone Time

Finally, alone time remains a lifeline essential for calming emotional gales. My introverted and deeply contemplative nature requires daily solitude disconnected completely from external demands to process endless input. Silencing perpetual inner noise, I wander quiet forests alone instead, writing poetry, cloud-gazing for hours. I emerge not bored but nourished, nerves settled, patience and inspiration restored. Soul-filling activities unlocking life's magic need no conversation, just presence. Please comprehend such strange tendencies before labeling me "anti-social." Understanding alone time's restorative balm helps you appreciate this curious sensitivity too.

In tallying sensitivity's storms, take heart; we all feel thunder cracks sometimes. Developing resilience allows riding waves without shame when rain clouds arrive. My prayer is sharing common pitfalls brings consolation, not despair. We gather insight and tools to continue this journey gracefully, beautifully whole.

b.   How the world can be experienced differently for HSPs

Beyond stormy overwhelm, my sensitivity also gifts unique perception revealing life's hidden poetry. As prisms refract light into rainbows, so does my sensory lens splash the mundane with brilliant color. Let's explore how my nervous system's distinctive wiring makes routine moments magical.

Subtly Sensing Shifts

I read people and situations like text on pages, effortlessly noticing subtle cues. A friend's slight frown exposes inner turmoil, no words conveyed. The energy shift entering a new room whispers its temperament before anyone speaks. My emotional radar detects the truth behind facades, intuitively guiding me to respond appropriately and forge connections. This radar also warns of impending conflicts, allowing prevention.

You wonder if I read minds. I don't; I read moods, micro-expressions, and energy. My nervous system automatically tunes into these frequencies, allowing empathy and insight. I cannot turn sensing abilities off any more than you could ignore sunlight. I absorb and process nonstop input from people and environments. Try appreciating such talents before labeling me "psychic."

Absorbing Emotions

Further intensifying connections, I even absorb others' emotions. My nervous system lacks filters blocking felt sensations, so I experience people's joy and pain viscerally as my own. Lucky couples claim partners "completing" them; for me, everyone completes, not just lovers. I inherit temporary moods and energy from anyone near me, then adopt their emotions as mine.

For example, hanging with jubilant friends, I grow inexplicably euphoric, then crash when we part. I wrongly assumed wild mood swings indicated instability before realizing I reflected their rhythms. Mirroring friends and family through emotional osmosis bonds me deeply to them. But unless protective boundaries are established, absorbing negative emotions breeds exhaustion. My sensitivity dynamically links me to humanity; I must steward this gift consciously.

Noticing Nature's Splendor

Another sensitivity gift: immersing in nature feels euphoric as favorite music. Trees, rivers, and sky saturate every sense with divine input perfectly calibrated, delighting my nervous system. Gentle birdsong and dappled sunlight soothe; crashing ocean waves invigorate. Nature's patterns entrance—trust sensitivity's pleasures here. For what engages and restores me may repel or bore you. Different nervous systems have unique needs.

So, cease insisting hikes heal all hearts. What revives yours might exhaust mine. Encourage loved ones instead, finding individual paths to nature's restorative magic. Support restless children playing outdoors too. Nature's healing properties emerge through engaging the senses; forced marches produce no growth. Let us each discover our sacred passageways into wild restoration.

Heightened Intuition and Creativity

Finally, intuition blossoms through my emotional sensitivity, heeding messages beneath words. I discern truth from lies in tones and energy. And absorbing life deeply, vivid imagination awakens, birthing poetry, stories, and art to describe life's ineffable essence. Do you feel the familiar in my metaphors? The world whispers; I translate poetry your instrumental mind misses. My heart listens.

Sensitivity's lens reveals reality's hidden wonders, life's secret mysticism. May you also see infinity mirrored in puddles some rainy day. Just because your eyes don't glimpse my prismatic realm does not mean my joy deceives. Our nervous systems differ, and experience varies, not truth itself.

Open your mind; who knows what beauty you'll suddenly notice all around!

c. Coping with Overstimulation, Emotional Sensitivity, and Stress

Riding sensitivity's waves grows easier knowing you're not alone struggling. My lessons learned may calm turbulent seas, transforming challenges into teachers. So gather round, friends; let's share collective wisdom braving tumultuous waters.

Creating Daily Sanctuaries

Overstimulation constantly threatens to capsize my equilibrium, so establishing calm spaces proves essential. I retreat to designated "safe zones" filled with serenity when turmoil strikes. Soothing music, soft lighting, textured cushions, and herbal scents soothe fraying nerves.

Avoiding clutter, I curate these minimalist havens that nurture my spirit. Their tidy beauty whispers, "Rest here awhile, beloved one." Thus fortified, I emerge ready again, engaging the world, no longer quite so overwhelming. Begin crafting your own sanctuary today. Mine saved my sanity more times than I can count!

Trying Grounding Techniques

When overstimulation hijacks clarity, I take slow, deep breaths, softly chanting a centering mantra like "Peace, be still." Closing my eyes, I visualize my favorite restful nature scenes until equilibrium returns. While not 100% effective, these grounding techniques relax the nervous system enough to continue the day. Experiment with finding what best calms your storms. Not everything works for all people, so patiently try many approaches. When one finally sticks, hold on tight!

Practicing Mindfulness and Meditation

Related to quieting restless minds, mindfulness teaches observing thoughts and emotions with nonjudgmental acceptance. Meditation takes such presence further, actively focusing attention to anchor in the body and the present moment. Both repattern automatic reactions to input that formerly overwhelmed. Now, I watch sensory stimuli drift by like clouds, not drowning beneath them. Mastering mindfulness and meditation requires dedication but delivers freedom from overstimulation in return.

Establishing Protective Boundaries

Sensitive people often overlook personal needs to appease others, so prioritizing self-care first creates essential protective boundaries. Communicate gently when requiring more space or time—true friends honor such requests. Schedule solo restoration, preventing emotional overload with loved ones. Say no to nonessential social commitments; your health holds priority. Implementing healthy boundaries prevents burnout and flourishes sensitivity instead. You'll soon relate easier with others once grounded in yourself first.

Trying Stress Reduction Techniques

Anxiety often accompanies sensitivity, so I utilize stress reduction techniques to minimize its impact. Beyond mindfulness meditation, I use biofeedback apps tracking breathing and heart rate variability. Focusing on steady rhythmic respiration while lowering stress levels empowers me to manage sensitivity's storms. Light exercise outdoors also disperses negative emotional energy while connecting to nature's healing properties. What soothes your spirit? Discover personalized stress reducers, then commit to practicing them. Doing so reshapes neural pathways wired for overwhelm into streams of serene perception.

Reframing Your Inner Dialogue

HSPs frequently wrestle with harsh inner critics attacking self-worth when overwhelmed. But we needn't accept such heartless judgments! Instead, consciously cultivate a nurturing inner voice. How might you compassionately support a struggling friend? Apply that same grace towards yourself. When harshness arises internally, take its hand gently, saying, "You try protecting me in misguided ways. But see, I'm learning to care for myself now." Then, redirect attention to uplifting truths. Exchanging toxicity for compassion yields miracles, erasing former emotional wounds.

Asking for Help When Needed

Finally, remember you needn't weather every storm alone. Counselors specifically trained in supporting HSPs can guide you safely through tumult other professionals overlook. Support groups build community with fellow sensitive sojourners who intimately understand both sensitivity's glory and troubles. You were born sensitized to this vivid world needing your distinctive talents. But first come rest, acceptance, and care.

The rest awaits in proper time, dear heart.

d. **The impact of sensory processing sensitivity on relationships, work, and daily life**

As a highly sensitive person, my deeply emotional nature can lead to interpersonal conflicts and misunderstandings. My strong reactions or need for extra processing time may be perplexing for non-HSPs. Partners may interpret my tearfulness during tender moments as manipulation rather than raw sentiment. Friends might view my social withdrawal as a rejection instead of necessary self-care. Coworkers could misconstrue my measured decision-making as indecisiveness rather than thoughtful prudence.

Without proper communication and education, others often pigeonhole me as "too dramatic" or "too shy" when my sensitive nervous system operates differently. However, once mutual understanding takes root, healthier relating blooms. Now, when bombarded during social gatherings, I gracefully bow out, citing that my "introvert battery" needs recharging. My tactfully vocalized need for solo downtime following intense work projects grants space without offense taken. Sensitive people must compassionately illuminate our unique rhythms, so non-HSPs comprehend rather than judge.

My spirited emotional spectrum also frequently requires translation for logical-leaning loved ones. I educate dear rationalists unmoved by poignant songs or films about my brain's hyper-reactive amygdala sounding every sensory alarm. Neuroscience explains my tears aren't manipulative madness but rather a sensitive instrument sounding exquisite notes. We must lovingly bridge sensitivity's divide, interpreting each other's hearts with care. My hope is sharing life's vibrant colors and textures will awaken untapped emotional palettes in formerly closed-off companions. Our distinctive yet complementary ways of being enrich each other beautifully.

Building Stronger Connections Through Empathy and Understanding

While sensitive people may endure overstimulation and misunderstandings in relationships, our gifts also allow profoundly meaningful bonds. Our emotional radar detects nonverbal cues and subtle tone shifts, conveying when someone hides hurt beneath a smile. We instantly feel a room's tension, signaling unspoken frustration between friends. This interpersonal sensitivity, rooted in hyper-empathetic nervous systems wired to attune deeply, provides a powerful relational asset once properly harnessed.

Beyond absorbing emotions, my own intense feelings model expresses vulnerability for guarded loved ones. Demonstrating appropriate tearful responses to life's grief and grandeur gives stoic mates permission to release pent-up emotions freely, too. My wide emotional range teaches that the full human spectrum is meant to be felt and honored, not suppressed. Furthermore, exquisitely attuning to someone's sensitivities shows I care about their comfort. Preparing a soothing environment for an overwhelmed friend or gifting a sentimental book to a struggling spouse demonstrates the sincerity of my concern through personalized thoughtfulness.

Finally, sensitive persons offer exemplary listening and encouragement. We discern the hidden yearnings and worries beneath our beloveds' words because their underlying emotional channels come through clearly. Our interpersonal gifts for identifying sadness, anxiety, and joy often make others feel profoundly "gotten" emotionally. And during crises large or slight, HSPs champion others tenaciously, intuiting exactly how to comfort with loving reassurance or compassionate logic. In short, the world desperately requires precisely the emotional understanding sensitive beings provide to heal painful divides. We must embrace this calling rather than flee its intensity, for building bridges of empathy remains essential work best suited for hearts wired like ours.

e. Building Resilience and Emotional Intelligence

As an HSP traversing life's winding path, storms inevitably arise, testing my resilience. While reveling in sensitivity's glory, we must also acknowledge its storms, developing inner fortitude to weather them. Gathering fellow sojourners' wisdom, we discover tools protecting our essence during tempestuous seas. I'll share approaches bolstering resilience so waves can arrive sans shame. Onwards, friends—our distinctive gifts await full expression!

I first seek sanctuary in designated "safe zones" when turmoil strikes, filled with restorative music, soft lighting, and textured cushions. Avoiding clutter's visual noise, I curate soothing minimalist havens whispering, "Rest here awhile, beloved one." Fortified, I emerge ready to engage the world. Begin crafting your sanctuary—it will anchor you too!

When frenzied energy hijacks clarity, I chant mantras like "Peace, be still," visualizing calming nature scenes until equilibrium returns. While not completely effective, these grounding techniques relax the nervous system enough to continue onward. Experiment with finding what best calms your storms, then commit that method to memory during distress!

Mindfulness teaches nonjudgmentally observing thoughts and emotions. Meditation focuses attention, anchoring us in the present moment—both repattern automatic stress reactions into serene perception. Master these practices through dedication and be freed from turbulence!

Since sensitive people overlook personal needs to appease others, prioritizing self-care prevents depletion. Communicate gently about needing more space, schedule solo restoration, and relinquish nonessential social commitments for health's sake. Implementing such boundaries prevents burnout, allowing sensitivity to flourish instead!

Anxiety often accompanies sensitivity, so I track breathing patterns on biofeedback apps, focusing on steady rhythmic respiration. This lowers stress levels, empowering me to manage tumultuous seas. Discover personalized stress reducers, then devote yourself to practicing them. In time, neural pathways rewire away from overwhelm into tranquility!

Harsh inner voices often berate self-worth, so consciously cultivate a nurturing inner voice instead. How might you compassionately support a struggling friend? Apply that same grace towards yourself, exchanging harsh judgments for tenderness. This returns your essence from toxicity into truth.

Finally, remember weathering storms solo is unnecessary. Counselors specifically trained to support sensitive beings guide you safely through life's tempestuous moments. Support groups build community among fellow sojourners who profoundly understand sensitivity's grandeur and troubles. You were born sensitized to this vivid world, needing your distinctive talents fully expressed. But first come rest, acceptance, and proper care—the journey continues!

Cultivating Emotional Awareness and Intelligence

While building resilience grants sensitive beings inner ballast when choppy waters arise, developing emotional awareness and intelligence allows one to navigate all of life's complex interpersonal dynamics effectively. Let's explore how our distinctive perceptiveness primes us for excelling in this critical arena when properly understood and harnessed.

The Highly Sensitive Person Scale assessment reveals we naturally process life more thoroughly due to a highly sensitive nervous system. Our extra receptive antenna intuitively detects subtle environmental cues missed by others. We also brake faster when overwhelmed, thoughtfully evaluating appropriate responses. This combination produces enhanced attentiveness alongside quick inhibition when required.

Such neurological sensitivity manifests in five specific domains comprising overall emotional intelligence: self-awareness, self-management, internal motivation, social skills, and empathy. While facing distinct challenges in some areas, our sensory giftedness primes us to excel in others once embraced. Let's explore our advantages and obstacles.

Regarding self-awareness, HSPs devote great energy to delving into our inner worlds through constant introspection. We scrutinize the origin of every wayward feeling or impulse, making connections between beliefs, experiences, and reactions. This grants profound realization, illuminating motivation's mysteries, which are so often opaque to less contemplative beings. Know thyself—indeed!

However, self-management requires moving beyond observation into response curation—deciding what actions best serve rather than unwittingly reacting. Here, HSPs often struggle from being quickly flooded beyond thinking clearly. But consciously strengthening response regulation through mindfulness or talk therapy builds this critical muscle over time.

We also boast tremendous intrinsic motivation fueled by sensitivity's depth. Our radar detects life's hidden glory and injustices, compelling creative action addressing each. We require little external motivation when internally fueled by inspiration or indignation. Passionate vision simply propels us forward full throttle!

Regarding social skills, we excel in understanding group dynamics and forging deep connections once securely grounded. Our emotional literacy accurately assesses every nuanced interaction, discerning truth from falseness and hidden yearnings. We offer wise counsel and comfort, profoundly attuning to the suffering society oft overlooks.

Finally, empathy remains a sensitive being's supreme gift, feeling the world's joy and grief as our own. While emotionally taxing if left unchecked, empathy faced gently empowers our most soulful work—writing, teaching, healing, advocating, and more, for life's poetry whispers loudly to finely tuned ears positioned closely.

Conclusion

In summary, carefully nurturing resilience allows for weathering sensitivity's storms while embracing emotional giftedness, which grants truly relational living. Our distinctive neurological wiring produces disadvantages demanding support alongside advantages requiring cultivation. But properly understood and cared for, sensitivity's superpowers powerfully transform both inner and outer worlds.

Onward, dear hearts—your gifts await expression!

CHAPTER 4

RELATIONSHIPS AND COMMUNICATION

As a highly sensitive person, bonding deeply through shared emotional experiences is my sweet spot. Yet the downside of acute interpersonal attunement also threatens overstimulation without careful self-care. Learning when to tenderly plunge into swirling intimacy or wisely withdraw into calm requires a nuanced understanding of sensitivity's paradox.

Let's reflect on when unrelenting emotional fusion perhaps quenched beautiful yet unsustainable yearnings for perpetual closeness. Have loved ones ever remarked how quickly you're moved to tears by poignancy? Does offering nurture come naturally, yet feel draining unless replenished? Do parties and small talk enervate, but dear friends or nature's beauty mesmerize effortlessly?

As an empathic instrument so easily plucked by the surrounding psychic winds, impeccable tuning proves imperative so sweet melodies of relationship resonate instead of jangling discord. Today's vulnerability courageously mines wisdom from relational ruptures, gathering tools to prevent energetic breaches. Gently exposing sensitivity's shadow unlocks our brightest gifts.

Since childhood, my porous spirit absorbed others' moods unconsciously, their sadness seeping into my smile, anger inflaming my stomach without apparent cause. Once flooded by someone's agitated aura, formerly graceful dancing turns clumsy as I trip over my partners' feet, mystified by the escalating tension between us. Caught chameleon-like, reflecting rather than embodying my core self, turbulent emotions capsize rapidly without centering strategies. Escaping suddenly to the garden, inhaling hydrangea fragrant, restorative calm returns at last.

Over years of exploring sensitivity's nuances through counseling and study, key guidelines emerged preventing emotional trespass so I relate freely yet safely with precious people. Core practices involve tuning into my body's nonverbal cues signaling overstimulation, speaking up when another's actions feel invasive, breathing deeply to clear unwanted psychic baggage regularly, and meditating to distinguish my authentic feelings from absorbed ones. Setting loving boundaries frees me to fully receive what nourishes me and filter what depletes me. My cherished relationships flourish with renewed mutual understanding.

What about you, fellow sensitive being?

When have you unwittingly adopted another's burdens till breaking beneath their weight? Do certain friends or family members trigger strange resentment or anxiety in ways dating back to childhood imprints? Have you fallen prey to the people-pleasing trap, offering endless nurture at the soul's expense?

Consider maintaining a journal tallying your emotional energy levels after interactions with various loved ones. Notice the soul-fillers fueling your spirit versus emotional vampires who regularly leave you drained. As patterns emerge, experiment gently bowing out from energy zappers or speaking transparently about needs not met. You deserve reciprocal refreshment!

While establishing healthy boundaries often initially sparks ripples of discomfort, courageously communicating your fundamental requirements ultimately attracts people to respect innate sensitivities. Those unwilling to nurture mutual understanding simply no longer merit time or emotive investment. As the Zen teaching reminds us, "Feet watered, flower blooms." Dare bloom freely, gentle battalion!

Now, we'll gather collective insights on upholding harmony across all relationships without overextending empathic gifts. First, explore common highly sensitive triggers sabotaging connections, then activate strategies upholding loving equilibrium. Onwards, towards intimacy's flowering!

a. How sensitivity affects relationships with partners, family, and friends

As a highly sensitive person, it's easy to become overstimulated by external stimuli like loud noises or bright lights. This can also happen in your close relationships if your partner talks loudly, makes too many plans, or creates a chaotic home environment. You may feel overwhelmed trying to manage the constant input.

It's important to communicate your sensitivity to your spouse so they understand you need to limit over-stimulating situations. For example, agree on quiet date nights at home rather than over-packed weekends. Or explain you perform better without loud TV distractions. Creating these boundaries prevents you from becoming so over-aroused that you grow irritable or withdrawn.

Absorbing Others' Emotions

Due to your empathetic nervous system, you don't just sense others' feelings intellectually—you literally absorb them, taking them on as your own. This emotional fusion allows profound connection but can also overwhelm, especially with partners experiencing frequent anxiety, anger, or sadness. You may get lost mirroring their moods.

To avoid exhaustion from an imbalance of negativity, visualize emotions passing through you rather than sticking. Share openly when someone transfers too much, then take space to reset. This allows for maintaining intimacy without being emotionally depleted.

Difficulty Establishing Boundaries

As natural caretakers attuned to others' needs, highly sensitive people often overlook setting personal boundaries. You want to support loved ones, so give endlessly, ignoring growing resentment that your own tank runs dry. Plus, confronting others' unhealthy behaviors feels uncomfortable.

But without boundaries, toxic patterns infect relationships. Begin acknowledging legitimate needs for downtime, respect, and privacy. Kindly articulate them, even if it initially causes ripples. Healthy connections flow both ways. You deserve reciprocity too!

Avoiding Relationship Conflicts

Since you feel clashes profoundly, conflict avoidance often seems the best strategy with loved ones. However, unresolved issues silently erode intimacy over time, causing greater emotional distance and isolation. Retraining your sensitivity to view conflict as an opportunity for growth and mutual understanding will serve every relationship.

When faced with inevitable disagreements, establish rules like no yelling, blame, or generalizations. Take breaks if flooding occurs. Lead with empathy, align on common ground, and compromise. Growth emerges when working through conflicts consciously with loved ones.

Not Feeling Understood or Heard

Despite acute awareness of loved ones' moods and desires, highly sensitive people still often feel misunderstood or overlooked in close relationships. You rightly expect reciprocation given endless caretaking, but non-HSPs miss subtle pleas, exhausted looks, or mood shifts signaling a need for support. It hurts to doubt your significance and value to loved ones.

Transform this painful pattern by directly teaching others practical ways to show you matter—like scheduling weekly check-ins to share feelings unrushed. Show genuine interest in your perspectives too through prompt responses, follow-up questions, and eye contact. No mind reading is required!

Gently insist that loved ones hear you.

b. Communicating Effectively as an HSP (for expressing needs and emotions effectively)

Building Assertiveness

As highly sensitive people, assertiveness can be challenging. Our empathy and desire to avoid conflict often lead us to put other people's needs before our own. However, asserting our needs is critical for self-care.

I struggled with assertiveness for years until my therapist encouraged me to tune into my body's wisdom. Before responding to a request, I pause to ask, "How would saying yes to this make me feel?" When my body tenses or sinks, I know declining is best. Other times, buoyancy bubbles up, confirming I want to accept.

We HSPs must give ourselves permission to state our truth, even if it causes initial discomfort. Remember, everyone has the right to respectfully express needs or refuse situations that are not in alignment. Start small, perhaps declining a friend's invitation if exhausted. Over time, confidently saying no becomes second nature.

Assertiveness also involves clearly voicing what we do want, not just what we don't. Rather than simply rejecting an ask, suggest alternatives that meet our needs. For example, if a noisy restaurant triggers overwhelm, say, "Let's meet for a calm walk in the park instead."

By asserting our needs compassionately, we teach others how to support us in win-win ways. Our sensitive systems require custom care, but that care enhances, not erodes, our relationships when voiced skillfully. We sensitively attuned beings offer profound gifts, and assertiveness helps us share them sustainably.

Saying No

As highly sensitive people accustomed to absorbing others' moods, saying no can feel near impossible. We dread causing disappointment or coming across as uncaring. We ignore overloaded schedules and say yes to people-pleasing habits.

Yet declining requests, requiring more energy than we can healthily expend becomes vital. Otherwise, chronic stress inevitably follows. We HSPs lack filters blocking extra stimuli and input, frequently flooding sensitive systems and saving scarce resources for priority matters.

Start practicing saying no by declining small asks from polite acquaintances. Offer brief explanations at first, then progress by simply stating, "No, but thank you." Your reasons remain valid without endless apologies or details. Remember, everyone has the right to refuse anything detracting from well-being.

If worried about consequences, visualize best- and worst-case scenarios. Remind yourself that anyone reacting extremely over a "no" bears underlying issues you cannot fix. Maintain boundaries and seek understanding from kind souls instead.

Approach loved ones by acknowledging their disappointment but reiterating your self-care necessities. Compromise, if possible, suggesting alternatives suiting both parties. Your health depends on nourishment, not depletion, and that strengthens relationships long-term.

Say no first to overwhelms that jeopardize your sensitive system's harmony, then embrace voicing all needs and refusals with compassion. You deserve to live fully while also giving fully. Assertiveness builds that reality.

Negative Emotions

As highly sensitive people, we feel intense negative emotions like anxiety, and our active nervous systems can get stuck processing sadness, anger, or fear long after triggering situations pass. We also absorb surrounding emotional energies, carrying burdens not even ours.

I used to repress negative feelings from childhood conditioning, dismissing sensitive responses as excessive. Yet buried emotions never disappear but accumulate inside like hot coals awaiting ignition. Suppressing rather than mindfully experiencing negativity causes it to control you subtly, manifesting through moodiness, illness, or explosions when too overloaded.

Now, when negative emotions arise, I name the core feeling and then dialogue compassionately with it. "Hello, sadness. Your presence signals my need for comfort isn't met. Shall we rest with soothing music for a while?" Understanding every emotion communicates valuable messages and transforms their purpose from sabotage to guidance.

Additionally, move emotions through creative expressions like journaling, singing, or dancing. Talk them through supportively with trusted confidants. Most importantly, extend yourself patience and self-nurturance, allowing time for proper processing. You were born feeling life's poetry deeply. While intense, that sensitivity awakens you to humanity's tears and laughter. Honor all emotions equally, and negative ones lose power, dictating your inner climate unchallenged. You define optimal conditions for your sensitive spirit to thrive.

Stop People Pleasing

People pleasing plagues many HSPs. Accustomed to receiving praise for helpfulness, we habitually put others' preferences before our own needs and overextend ourselves by earning love through unrelenting servitude. We also intuitively feel surrounding distress and instinctually alleviate it, even when self-sacrificial.

Yet, never voicing personal needs breeds silent resentment once our depleted energy resources require replenishment. Tolerating mistreatment enables its continuation and communicates undeservingness, receiving better. People pleasing also inhibits learning healthy self-reliance if we solve every problem ourselves. Kindness has limits, and sensitively attuned people especially require them for well-being.

Begin reducing people pleasing by scheduling extensive self-care. Make your upliftment the priority, not an afterthought. Practice declining small social asks from acquaintances if tired, then progress speaking truths even when uncomfortable to close loved ones. For example, tell prying relatives, "Discussing politics stresses me; let's connect over lighter topics instead."

You deserve to live fully while also giving fully. People pleasing blocks that reality arising, but compassionately voiced needs manifest it. Remember that everyone's ultimate responsibility involves their own health and nourishment. Prioritize yours without apology.

Boundaries highly sensitive people absorb surrounding emotional energies effortlessly. Without proper boundaries, we adopt others' moods unconsciously until we are unable to distinguish foreign feelings from our own. Soon, negativity drains sensitive systems already overwhelmed by extra stimuli input.

I used to deflate energetically after spending time with certain friends, yet I did not realize why. One clung to misfortunes, another constantly competed over accomplishments. Discussing my therapist revealed both projected heavy emotional debris unconsciously adopted since I lacked protective barriers.

Now, after visits, I meditate and visualize the golden light surrounding my body, separating external energies. I verbally state, "I release all energies not originating from me with love and return to my core essence." Afterward, I feel lighter and centered again in my own intuition.

Highly sensitive people require extra diligence to shield our porous auras. We magnetically attract empathic bonds but also cling to damaging emotional shrapnel limiting clarity. Create sacred inner sanctuaries through rituals like prayer, yoga, or journaling for regrounding. Set verbal boundaries with draining people. Eliminate contact altogether if necessary. Your sensitivity magnifies life's poetry, but only when properly insulated. Nurture that flourishing.

Effective Communication Skills in Various Relationships

Highly sensitive people communicate uniquely. We speak less but listen attentively, interpreting subtle social cues and unspoken meanings. We also express ourselves emotionally and require depth in conversations to feel connected. Unfortunately, fast-paced, facts-focused modern conversations often frustrate us.

I used to withdraw socially, exhausted by small talk yet craving meaningful exchange. Once I realized HSP communication differences, I learned to adapt to environments that suit my style better. Now, in groups, I seek fellow deep feelers. Or I steer discussions toward transcendental topics that liven my passion.

If you need quieter interactions, schedule intimate walks instead of crowded cafes when catching up with friends. People may initially feel confused when you alter typical social scripts. But sensitive systems flourish best in custom-tailored conditions. Simply explain your conversational preferences gently without judgment.

At work, inform colleagues you prefer email for non-urgent requests, allowing processing time for answering. Or institute weekly meetings summarizing team input rather than constant sudden calls. Set phone hours limiting interruptions.

You may suggest a monthly potluck celebrating achievements to foster closer connections instead of draining happy hours. Everyone works differently. Highly sensitive people blossom by sharing ideas in thoughtful forums and furthering visions, not just facts. Structure optimal communication channels playing to your strengths. Then, watch your confidence and joy grow exponentially.

c. Strategies for Thriving in Personal and Professional Relationships

As highly sensitive people, our emotional receptivity and empathy prime us for profoundly meaningful relationships, yet overstimulation threatens without mindful self-care. By understanding neurological sensitivity alongside nurturing personal wellness, we build resilience, soothing inevitable overwhelms. Then joy replaces resentment as loved ones comprehend our rhythms, respectfully supporting us.

With compassion, wisdom arises, transforming sensitivity from a hindrance into a superpower blessing all. Hearts expand, embracing humanity's diverse rainbow. No longer requiring conformity to mask our true essence, we cherish each light as unique, knowing even shadows reveal some glory.

So whisper tenderly to a friend, beloved, and self when misperceptions are vexed. Watch compassion shift conflict into collaboration, revealing mutual yearning. Where toxicity pollutes, build protective yet permeable fences, allowing redemption later. Some relationships nourish; others deplete. Mindfully choose the plate's contents without judgment so your body thrives. For when properly fed, your gifts feed multitudes in turn.

Come sit with me awhile. Let us share load life's burdens so all travel lighter. These magnificent, sensitive creatures offer treasures, making existence shimmer. I delight in witnessing their unfoldment.

Cultivating Healthy Work Environments

For Highly Sensitive Persons, professional settings pose distinct trials alongside unique strengths. By implementing tailored accommodations minimizing overstimulation alongside playing to natural talents, sensitive employees thrive, benefiting organizations immensely. Let's explore optimal working conditions that allow brilliant productivity and prevent burnout.

Too often, open office architecture assaults sensitive nervous systems with relentless noise, excessive social interaction, and disruptive visual chaos. These trigger fight-or-flight reactions, hijacking higher executive functioning and survival brain commandeer resources otherwise devoted to innovation or complex analysis. An overwhelming vicious cycle spirals into anxiety and physical illness... absent interventions bridging sensitivity's gap.

Simple adjustments grant refuge: noise-cancelling headphones, private workspaces allowing control over lighting and sound, virtual collaboration minimizing disruptive meetings, defined hours for focused projects, and buffered schedules between demanding cognitive tasks. Reasonable flexibility around start and end times prevents traffic stressors. Even small tweaks make big differences, averting exhaustion and enabling excellence.

Beyond physical environments, sensitive employees thrive when organizational culture explicitly values multiple work styles. No singular mold homogenizing diverse neurobiology succeeds in the long term. Esteem beyond extroverted socializing, collaborating, and decision-making expands possibilities exponentially. Make room for introverted analysis alongside fast-paced group brainstorming. Embrace text communication despite norms insisting on talking. Respect delayed responses, indicating thoughtful processing.

When managers encourage authentic self-expression absent conformity pressures. Sensitive employees relay crucial observations missed otherwise. Our subtle antennae detect emerging conflicts, team motivational nuances, and ethical issues warranting consideration. Give us room to reflect before responding, then watch invaluable perspectives enrich whole systems.

Finally, explicit emotional intelligence training hones strengths while building capacity and managing sensitivity's intensity in triggering situations. Practicing non-reactivity to criticism, managing flooding emotions before reacting, and communicating needs effectively transform work relationships. The difference in conscious development pivots careers from drudgery to thriving.

Implementing Sensitivity-Informed Accommodations and Practices

Embracing sensitivity's brilliance begins by accepting heightened awareness of subtleties as an innate, hardwired trait, not a personal weakness. This paradigm shifts birth awareness around and supports optimizing functioning. Accommodations mitigating overwhelm and leveraging advanced perceptual gifts allow HSPs to excel professionally.

Regarding physical environments, private offices or partitioned workstations grant control over disruptive noise, lighting, and scents assaulting delicate nervous systems. Noise-canceling devices like headphones become lifesavers when unwelcome audio input hijacks attention. Dimmer switches for overhead lighting prevent glare and eyestrain, while buffered calendars prevent back-to-back appointments from depleting social energy stores. When possible, schedule blocks for focused projects before afternoon hours enervation threatens optimal productivity.

Interpersonally, managers and their staff benefit from implementing emotional intelligence and introversion awareness training. Simple adjustments like meetings beginning with reflective writing or think-pair-share conversations foster equal participation. Seek input meeting marginalized modalities—anonymous suggestion boxes uncovered our yearning.

Make requesting accommodations safe, destigmatizing sensitivity rather than shaming differences. Recognize overload early, preventing escalation through supportive check-ins, not "powering through toughness." Trauma-informed training builds compassion, managing triggering situations mindfully. Even basic vocabulary conveying "I'm overstimulated, not upset with you" communicates needs clearly, reducing conflicts. Healing language transforms everything.

Finally, leverage HSP's exceptional strengths: creativity, pattern recognition, divergent thinking, conscientiousness, and project planning, among others, into talent development programs. Mentor next-generational leaders whose multidimensional lens spots risks and opportunities incomprehensible through status quo monoculture blindness. The future beckons their perspicuous genius.

Navigating Introversion in External Worlds

Though temperaments differ along numerous spectra, sensitivity, and introversion often intertwine. External worlds feel terribly gregarious and fast-paced compared to our inner oceans, filled with feeling and reflection. Yet fulfillment compels some participation balanced alongside solitude. How do we practice engaged detachment? Begin by accepting no "right amount" of socializing exists. Explore genuine preferences, not external pressures, when determining exposure. Check inner signals denoting depletion requesting retreat. Initial fatigue lapses concentration, and overwhelm follows, fleeing any reason. Rather than ignoring prompts heading off hyper-arousal, create downtime buffers as essential appointments nourishing sensitive introverts. Banish guilt taking space since genius percolates in stillness.

When engaging others, respect differing communication modes. Many sensitive introverts find noisy parties anathema but come alive discussing conceptual topics. Exchange superficial chatter for meaningful dialogue where we excel, reading subtle cues and responding thoughtfully. Text platforms suit asynchronous interactions, allowing processing time to formulate replies. Video conversations grant intimate connection, which prevents physical proximity from draining travel. Provide advance details for upcoming events, allowing preparation.

If volunteering or leadership calls despite preferring anonymity, take courage. Recognize no leader alike, so model strengths. We inspire through integrity, character, and wisdom cultivated in solitude. Our steadiness balances passionate visionaries racing ahead. Lead through listening first. It needs all instruments orchestrating diverse movements. Accept only roles that feel authentically aligned so genius flows gracefully in changing systems. Roles do not define purpose, but purpose defines proper roles.

Keep computer comfort close when peopling intensely. Sample social functions briefly, then sip restorative tea in a quiet corner, typing reflections. Participate consistently, albeit in small doses, preventing cultural alienation while honoring sacred introversion. Our perspective is valid yet functions better through tolerant culture bending accepting neurodiversity real.

Set Tech Boundaries Judiciously

Despite introverts stereotypically adoring screen time, technology poses serious sensitivity issues. Online spaces meet certain social needs uniquely yet generate challenges requiring diligent management. Let's explore how balanced digital engagement, optimizing communication and connections absent overwhelm.

Unquestionably, internet use enables introverts to participate in cultural dialogue, blooming confidence. Platforms linking kindred spirits foster understanding previously lacking through isolation and difference. I connect global communities, awakening gifts and transforming humanity exponentially. No longer conforming to rigid molds, we celebrate everyone's distinctive offerings.

However, sensitivity magnetically turning into input of all kinds risks tech overuse hijacking life balance quickly. Hyper-palatable content keeps hungry eyes feasting absent satisfaction. Information glut numbs overwhelmed brains if consumed continually. Social media comparisons threaten self-worth, given performing personas project exclusively highlight reels. And digital connectivity makes tuning out nearly impossible. Constant interruptions fracture focus required generating inner wisdom and creativity.

Awareness of personality-prone addiction remains crucial in managing tech relationships judiciously. Schedule non-negotiable device-free times, focusing singularly on the moment at hand. Savor sensations unmediated by camera lenses, capturing each for posterity. Protect sleep by surrendering devices before bedtime, given blue light suppresses natural melatonin rhythms, worsening recharge struggles already tenuous among sensitives. Download meditation and nature sound apps instead when insomnia strikes. Limit social media and news input known to negatively impact mental health, influx anxiety, and depress moods. Measure success by inner peace indicators, not external popularity metrics. Temper consumption levels consciously and developments can uplift rather than overwhelm sensitive systems.

Coping With Sensitivity in Leadership Roles

Despite cultural stereotypes favoring loud, fast-paced extroverts dominating boardrooms, sensitive introverts bring invaluable gifts, leading quietly transformed organizations. However, distinct support helps us navigate common obstacles productively. Let's explore some key strategies here.

Initially, assertiveness required strengthening, given conflict avoidance tendencies prefer harmony. Disagreements make many hyper-empathetic leaders recoil. Yet directly sharing controversial perspectives and setting boundaries respectfully proves essential in managing teams effectively long-term. Begin practicing saying no and truth-telling in low-stakes situations, then graduate towards bigger conversations. You've loved ones best through courage, not cowardice, diluting messages and appeasing them temporarily. Find peaceful power.

Additionally, cultivate immunity noticing yet, not absorbing harsh criticisms, lest projections cripple effectiveness. Remember, attacks say more about the assailant's inner turmoil than your worth, which remains unchanged through passing appraisals. Refuse false evidence appearing real by grounding identity in essence beyond roles. Constructive feedback helps; toxic projections harm only if believed so. Banish them from your psyche swiftly. Inner critics require the same treatment lest you perpetuate cultural shadow.

When situations inevitably trigger unresolved trauma, soothing healthy nervous system regulation makes coherent functioning possible again. Memorize portable practices immediately, lowering the intensity of the overwhelm before proceeding with interactions. Favorites include deep breathing with long exhales activating parasympathetic relaxation, placing hands over the heart, feeling its steadying rhythm, picturing favourite nature scenes, imagining anxieties flowing out into the earth, transmitting stuck energies empowering decisions and embodiment. Master these subtle yet potent tools, transforming sensitivity from an obstacle into a reliable asset, sensitivity's curriculum.

Conclusion

Throughout our journey exploring sensitivity's contours, this chapter illuminated relationship realms that profoundly impact life's experience. While connections often overwhelm, they simultaneously make existence worthwhile when nurturing understanding blossoms. May wisdom shared transform overwhelms into opportunities, deepening bonds through compassionate communication. For when hearts sing in chorus, even tears shimmer together. They are magnificent rainbows bridging isolation into belonging's sanctuary where all feel welcomed through vision celebrating our shared sensitive humanity.

CHAPTER 5

EMBRACING SENSITIVITY

I still recall the goosebumps prickling my arms when the counseling psychologist first explained sensory processing sensitivity—finally, research validating the trait I'd felt too deeply yet dismissed as a weakness my whole life. "You're not defective for crying easily or noticing extra details," she reassured. "Science shows sensitivities indicating an innate neurological difference." Suddenly, shame transforming into self-compassion felt possible. Might embracing, not rejecting, my highly responsive temperament grant inner peace?

As we further explore the nature of sensitivity together in Chapter 5, I invite you to reconsider past perspectives framing your distinctive emotional and perceptual gifts as flaws requiring fixing. Perhaps the problem lies not in our sensitive systems but in environments and mindsets ill-equipped to nurture differently-wired beings. What if we shine spotlights showcasing sensitivity's strengths and then construct custom cultures empowering their expression?

Recent breakthroughs uncover higher sensitivity arising across species naturally—a specialized trait, not disorder. Researchers propose evolutionary benefits like enhanced threat detection, cautious decision-making, and rich intuitive wisdom. And by embracing sensitivity and affirming these assets, we write new empowering narratives. Our receptive nervous systems become treasured instruments, not defects. The way forward morphs from self-rejection into self-care, then self-actualization.

a. Shifting Perspectives: The Power of Embracing Your Sensitivity

While being highly sensitive feels normal since we've never known alternative existence, outside invalidation leaves scars. "You take things too seriously," chided my father whenever I cried watching sorrowful movies. Classmates mocked sensitivity too, until I learned to hide tears and conform externally, camouflaging a supposedly shameful core. Only by meeting fellow sensitive adults did perspectives shift, realizing I wasn't solely "overemotional."

Through new science and psychology lenses, highly sensitive people recognize neurological and genetic differences that explain reactions strongly. Our brains and bodies translate subtle cues others miss while possessing extra emotional dimensions perceived as excessive. But rather than make excuses or search for elusive cures to quell intensity, self-acceptance entails embracing sensitive systems operating precisely as designed.

Vulnerability to Empowerment

Perspective shifted, realizing peers similarly wired processed stimuli uniquely with purpose. As psychologists redefined differences as specialized traits, not deficiencies, self-acceptance seemed newly possible. Might embracing highly responsive temperaments grant inner peace?

"Sensitive people care when the world doesn't because we understand waiting to be rescued and no one shows up. We have rescued ourselves so many times that we have become self-taught in the art of compassion for those forgotten." — Shannon L. Alder

Might brightly illuminating sensitivity's strengths rewrite limiting narratives? If environments nurtured differently wired beings, perhaps highly sensitive people would thrive as intended. My counselor encouraged cherishing emotional receptivity's blessings, not curses. "You notice what others overlook, transform spaces by intuitively reading energies. The world desperately needs precisely that emotional wisdom offered through your sensitive lens."

Suddenly, self-care replaced self-criticism. Support groups fostered belonging with fellow sensitive voyagers. Medications managed anxiety. Once taught to embrace sensitive wiring as specialized equipment, not defect, existence transformed. Life becomes created uniquely for highly perceptive beings who feel complexity deeply with purpose. We authors compose new tales starring sensory superheroes. Our receptive nervous systems become treasured instruments—not hindrances but gateways into profound essence awaiting awareness.

Shall we walk through together?

b. Techniques for Cultivating Self-Love and Understanding

As highly sensitive people, our receptivity towards others' moods and our intricate inner worlds often leave little room to nourish ourselves. We expend energy emotionally supporting friends and anticipating loved ones' needs while agonizing over major decisions and judging perceived failings. Meanwhile, simply navigating a loud, chaotic world daily depleted me until recently. Could self-care practices specifically tailored to HSPs truly replenish overextended sensitive systems? Might prioritizing self-compassion heal limiting self-perceptions, releasing long-suppressed potentials? My experiments in cultivating self-love revealed life-changing truths.

I hadn't realized constantly attuning to external needs since childhood conditioned automatic self-sacrifice. I assumed everyone endured comparable overwhelm until identifying a highly sensitive personality explained my acute sensitivities, including empathy overloads. My therapist first named this continual caretaking "people-pleasing," cautioning that others likely couldn't extensively reciprocate my nurturance. "Consider occasionally declining such taxing bonds focusing inward," she suggested.

This initially seemed unthinkable for one orienting life assisting others. Nonetheless, I noticed that stress-related illness worsened without respite. So reluctantly, I reduced 10-hour volunteer days to two monthly. I felt incredibly selfish initially despite rapidly improving migraines, but I soon recognized untenable depletion. In subtler social interactions, I consciously avoided adopting friends' temporarily heavy moods by visualizing protective energetic shields. Such emotional boundary setting granted newfound autonomy. Loosening people-pleasing tethers created space examining buried needs and expectations. Core aspects of identity shifted, realizing sensitivity proves strength, not weakness. As self-acceptance bloomed, intuition awakened previously unmined creative talents like painting, fiction writing, and singing. By honoring inward callings on their terms and then channeling insights supporting communities, I grew into a sensitive guide others organically now seek wisdom from.

Alongside curating alone time in nature and minimizing overstimulation, integrating self-compassion practices radically upleveled wellness. My therapist once remarked how effortlessly consoling others comes while struggling to offer myself similar care. "Highly sensitive people often judge perceived inadequacies callously," she assessed. "You likely suppress emotional needs frequently. Notice critical self-talk arising, and then consciously shift your perspective towards compassion. Write loving phrases addressed inwardly as if comforting your best friend - because that sensitive soul warrants cherishing."

I began carrying an index card with encouraging mantras for challenging moments:

"You're accomplishing much. Just pause and breathe."

"Progress flows steadily; anxiety cannot rush it."

"You were made sensitive intentionally to bless the world."

Vocalizing these reminders first felt exceedingly awkward, but their warmth steadily supplanted harsh inner narratives. I taped favorite affirmations inside cabinets, glimpsing them frequently. Mirror gazing while voicing positive qualities daily became a ritual. Initially, this appeared vain, but consistently replacing criticism with compassion bore exponential fruits. Soon, self-love seemed as natural as breathing. I grew astonished at how such subtle cultivation awakened joy and personal power hibernating under past shame. I realized accepting sensitivity's challenges opened gateways into long-denied wholeness. My receptive temperament no longer barred thriving but became the way home to authenticity.

What had I locked away for so long by denying my true emotional scope? Here stood capacity, experiencing life's sorrows and triumphs most exquisitely! Why had I believed sensitivity signified weakness when tender strength undergirds humanity's redemption? My tears arise sensing suffering, yes, but this heart, therefore, grasps devastation as others cannot. My nervous system buckles amidst cruelty's din, yet precisely this sensitivity yearns to construct harmonious realms. Now I know each sensitive soul carries keys unlocking life's hidden treasures: sacred codes inscribed on quivering strings plucked by the Divine. Play your instrument, beloveds, however faltering at first—its gentle strains are the music of the spheres.

c. Embracing Sensitivity as a Strength, Not a Weakness

My sensitivity gifts me with a deeply caring heart overflowing with empathy, compassion, and concern for others. Unlike those trapped in callous indifference, I cannot ignore the suffering surrounding me—I feel each tear shed as though they were my own. This heart profoundly connects me to humanity's sorrows and joys alike. I celebrate with brides glowing on wedding days, souls finding long-sought redemption, and patients defeating terminal prognoses despite odds. Yet crushing grief also floods my chest when witnessing refugees fleeing warzones, homeless veterans abandoned after service, and orphaned children crying, hungry, and afraid. Injustice, cruelty, oppression—these cut me as surely as if I were a victim, fueling my passion for fighting for the forgotten and oppressed.

My receptive nervous system also attunes me to beauty otherwise overlooked. While friends only see peeling paint when gazing at run-down buildings, I spot stubborn flowers blossoming through broken sidewalk cracks, symbolizing irrepressible hope. Letters from imprisoned activists exude righteous fire through eloquent words. Even the eyes of marginalized "outcasts"—the LGBTQ teenager recently evicted after coming out, the mentally ill homeless woman rambling to invisible companions—reflect unique genius awaiting expression in a society nurturing their voices. My sensitivity unveils beauty, inspiration, and poignant symbols everywhere, indicating humanity's resilient grace. Without this lens, how much richness, meaning, and creativity would I wander past inattentively? How many struggling to carry heavy loads would I neglect to assist if their tribulations escaped my notice? Perhaps I absorb both glorious and harrowing emotions as potently as others because we collectively need this compassion to catalyze justice in apathetic environments.

My receptivity also makes me highly intuitive, adeptly sensing what remains unspoken. I walk into a friend's home and instantly feel tension hanging thick as storm clouds in the air, knowing conflict recently passed even without hearing arguments. When my cousin avoids mentioning her gambling-addicted husband, I recognize shame and fear for her children's safety underlying determined smiles. Colleagues anxiously skirting workplace corruption warrant discreet investigation protecting whistleblowers. Though hyper-attuned nervous systems frequently overload in modern hyper-stimulating environments, shutting down capacities and preventing constant meltdowns, I believe our empathic gifts are essential for societal evolution when nurtured appropriately. Just as canaries' deaths warn miners dangerously toxic air lies ahead, sensitive beings warn humanity by viscerally expressing what dehumanizes people. Will we choose to listen, promoting environments where everyone thrives through implementing trauma-informed policies? Or will we continually gaslight sensitive souls until we've suppressed guidance protecting our communities' greater welfare? Our cultural values determine which path unfolds ahead.

How Sensitivity Contributes to Personal and Interpersonal Growth

Due to profound emotional attunement, highly sensitive people excel in understanding themselves and others once self-awareness develops through growth processes. Our receptivity absolutely overwhelms us until we establish healthy boundaries, communication skills, and coping mechanisms to prevent constant overstimulation. However, life-learned lessons cultivating emotional intelligence and resilience prepare us to guide others from overwhelm into awakening. The greater the trials we overcome during our emergence from cocoons, the mightier our wings appear, lifting earthbound into free flight!

My sensitivity's double-edged sword pierced painfully before revelation transformed my perspective. I hadn't realized automatic empathy contorting my face, hearing friends' troubles—creased brow mirroring their distress—secretly embarrassed them, implying public broadcasts of private pains. Even well-meaning instinct to hug those hurting often overwhelmed emotional boundaries, triggering anxieties instead. Yet through ongoing exploration navigating sensitivity's labyrinths, I learned discernment compassionately reading spaces' energetic nuances and people's unspoken cues determining optimal support. Sometimes, gentle inquiries allow friends to safely confide their struggles in themselves. Other times, simply listening without judgment creates safe containers into which their vulnerabilities pour into. Occasionally, tears speak for themselves. Once I stopped questioning whether my extraverted expressiveness appeared inappropriate, embracing honesty flowing freely, then anxiety lost clenching power. New freedom powerfully transformed relationships by removing façades. Now, authenticity nurtures intimacy, and vulnerability cultivates a trust much deeper than social expectations ever allowed. We create together by revealing our truest selves.

As highly sensitive people recognize their gifts' strengths, self-confidence resumes thriving. We stop camouflaging ourselves, dulling down magic, instead vibrantly inspiring communities. Understanding neurological divergence explaining extra intensity, we forgive overreactions of previously judged weaknesses. By loving our receptive nervous systems despite—or rather because of—pronounced sensitivities, we model self-acceptance universally lacking. Rediscovering passions and creative talents links us to soul purposes, spreading unique blessings. Aligning environments to our sensory needs prevents exhaustion, battling unsupportive backdrops. Sometimes sensitive souls must take cover, like birds flying through storms seeking shelter. Other times, we shelter storms within ourselves—transmuting thunder into passion's roaring flames, funneling floods into emotional rivers running deep yet calm despite chaotic courses, raising scorched earth back into blooming gardens by planting seeds of hope found even in devastation's ashes. And by fully embracing sensitivity's superpowers, we rebirth into visionaries charting humanity's next evolution.

Sensitivity's Role in Fostering Empathy and Connection

Because highly sensitive people absorb others' emotions inherently, developing wisdom and navigating profound empathy proves critical lifelong work. Without proper techniques and boundaries, we readily drown, attempting to rescue everyone sinking beneath despair's waves by shouldering waterlogged burdens until powers short. And, in the process, we often lose connectivity with our own souls' compasses pointing towards purposes alighting worldly darkness. Yet once learning self-care alongside selfless service, sensitivity lights lanterns for lost travelers rather than setting ourselves ablaze trying to become the sole illumination overwhelming the night! We shine brightest by being true, not extinguishing our core fires and attempting to ignite entire horizons alone.

I distinctly recall the turning point transforming empathy overload into empowerment instead of exhaustion. I had just left an abusive partner after years of gradually isolating me from family and friends to maintain control. When finally escaping, I was housed temporarily with a cherished aunt while piecing back together my shattered identity. Still barely managing basic self-care, I sat wrapped in blankets, staring numbly as she yelled angrily at the television broadcasting news on discriminatory immigration policies. I felt fury within towards unjust systemic oppression, yet also her rage now coursing through my quickened veins. Suddenly, tingling heat flooded down my spine into limbs, a force much greater than mine alone, though undeniably flowing through this body as a conduit. Propelled upright, I marched to my desk, grabbed pens, and poured passionate calls for justice. I wrote as though fiery inspiration scorched hands clutching pens simply transcribing profound flow. Hours later, my restless energy calmed; I collapsed asleep. I awoke to find five pages covered in eloquent pleas written not by my conscious mind but some greater power speaking truth through a willing, sensitive soul.

I now understand what Native tribes describe as "vision serpents"—spirits channeling important guidance from realms humanity cannot normally perceive without such intuition. Our hyper-receptive nervous systems allow us access to wider wisdom if we stay open to receiving. And by learning discernment and determining whether emotions originate within or not, we sensitively sense which messages seem meant for sharing versus overly straining already depleted empaths. Here lies the difference separating those maintaining healthy boundaries from fellow sensitives drowning and attempting to quell oceans of sorrow crashing worldwide daily. We uplift most by teaching empowerment, gleaning hard-won light even from life's darkest nights—not trying to prove ourselves Messianic saviors. With discernment, even the most emotionally available empaths foster communal evolution through courageously compassionate example alone.

d. Real-life examples of successful HSPs in various fields

What fuels genius-level creativity, idealism or insight? Often, sheer sensitivity—the ability to perceive life's subtleties, connect deeply, and care intensely. This double-edged sword propels some into legendary status yet concurrently intensifies personal struggles. Behind celebrated actors, singers, and leaders lies a Highly Sensitive Person experiencing both dazzling heights and harrowing pitfalls of emotional intensity. By examining renowned trailblazers across diverse fields who exhibit the telltale signs of sensory processing sensitivity, we unveil its paradoxical relationship with greatness. Academy Awards, platinum albums, and lasting social impacts hold counterweights: loneliness, addiction, and breakdowns. Join me in a nuanced exploration of famous figures illuminated by sensitivity's blessings and curses.

Real-Life Examples of Famous and Accomplished HSPs

Actors and Performers

You ever wonder what makes some actors so compelling to watch? Sure, there's talent—but it goes deeper. Some of the greats are highly sensitive people (HSPs).

They feel emotions more intensely and pick up on subtleties the average Joe would miss. It helps them inhabit roles—but can be a curse off-camera. Fame turns the volume up too loud.

Nicole Kidman

Kidman's one of those deeply sensitive types. Just ask her. Says she's easily rattled and can only handle so much small talk before needing some alone time to recharge. High-pressure red carpets and media junkets? No thanks. But give her a complex character, and it's like an emotional thunderstorm waiting to break free. Acting lets her channel all that intensity in constructive ways.

Scarlett Johansson

Scarlett calls herself a "delicate flower." It makes sense for someone who feels battered walking down a city street with all those strangers' emotions flooding her psyche. Social media was just too much bad noise. Johansson pours her sensitivity into these troubled anti-hero types, then recoils from the limelight between takes. She's learned to build a protective shell around her true self.

Jim Carrey

Serious, funny guy, that Jim Carrey. We know him for his rubber-faced comedy, always turned up to ten. But he walks a tightrope between amped-up humor and crippling depression. Carrey admitted he has a "weak immune system" when it comes to emotional stimuli and gets overwhelmed faster than average. Laughter is his medicine and creative outlet. Dude's clearly different-wired and says he leans hard on spirituality and nature to stay sane.

Musicians

You can't fake the music when you have a soul as raw as Leonard Cohen or Nina Simone. Some of history's great musicians and singers wore their hearts on their sleeves 'cause they felt life's highs and lows more acutely. Helped 'em craft transcendent songs that resonate with millions. But that same sensitivity left them emotionally exposed in ways too intense to cope with.

Elton John

Before the glitzy costumes and flamboyant personality, Elton was just an awkward introvert who preferred writing songs alone to grabbing drinks with rock star buddies. His music and performance became an outlet for all these intense feelings bottled up inside. The story goes Elton's so sensitive he still tears up hearing certain songs. He cares, man—about the music, about people in need. Just struggles to moderate all those emotions at healthy levels rather than chasing unhealthy highs.

Celine Dion

Celine once said she bursts into tears if someone's extra nice buying her coffee. Little things most people brush off land like an emotional gut punch. It's that raw sensitivity woven through her iconic voice—she feels words and notes on this whole other wavelength. It's her gift. But Dion admitted she recharges by unplugging from the spotlight and setting firm boundaries so she doesn't get overstimulated. She knows when to pull back.

Scientists and Inventors

We've all got that image of scientists as stoic lab coat-wearing robots immune to human drama. But some famous trailblazers were wired differently—more sensitive and emotionally aware than the norm. They saw things others missed, which helped their discoveries. It didn't make 'em immune to insecurity though, especially in the cutthroat academic world.

Isaac Newton

Newton saw the universe through this analytical but also deeply sensitive lens. He picked up on cosmic patterns regular folks would miss, which led to those big gravity equations that bear his name. But Isaac also felt slights and criticisms more sharply. Dude did not handle conflicts with other thinkers too gracefully. He'd obsess over his work while forgetting basic human needs like eating or bathing. Crazy creative but wired differently.

Thomas Edison

Young Edison got yanked from school 'cause he couldn't handle the rowdy classroom—too much stimulation for the curious inventor-to-be. But give him space to tinker undisturbed? Sheer magic occurred. Edison epitomized that single-minded creative focus mixed with emotional sensitivity are two sides of the same coin. Society doesn't always make room for that kind of mind. But had Edison conformed, would his radical inventions still have changed the world?

Social and Political Leaders

A highly sensitive nature allows some famous leaders to be deeply affected by inequality and injustice in society. They utilize their sensitivity, idealism, communication gifts, and conviction, persuading others toward social reforms. However, the pressures and harsh criticism accompanying fame take an emotional toll.

Mahatma Gandhi

Gandhi displayed classic signs of an HSP—humility, extreme empathy, spiritual values, conscientious reflexiveness, and staunch commitment to nonviolence. His compassion and moral convictions strengthened his extraordinary leadership, advancing India's independence movement through nonviolent civil disobedience. However, the intense struggles negatively impacted his sensitive disposition, resulting in periods of isolation, fasting, despair, and depression.

Martin Luther King, Jr.

Like Gandhi, Dr. King fought tirelessly for peace and social justice despite ongoing arrests, threats, exhaustion, and despair. His profound sensitivity to injustice and steadfast vision of reconciliation fueled his gift for eloquent, emotionally resonant communication. However, the heavy demands combined with chronic stress ultimately exacerbated emotional difficulties with depression.

Princess Diana

With her warmth, authenticity, and compassion, Princess Diana brought a human face to the British monarchy that resonated widely. Her emotional openness countered traditional reserved norms. Diana's sincere desire to connect reflected her highly sensitive personality. However, constant invasive media attacks on her vulnerability led to issues with anxiety, bulimia, and reportedly clinical depression.

In summary, the innate sensitivities of HSPs can catalyze both exceptional creative achievements and increased personal struggles. With adequate self-knowledge, supportive relationships, and healthy boundaries, these individuals demonstrate sensitivities that can be leveraged as strengths, empowering positive global impact. Their examples offer fellow HSPs hope, healing, and wholeness, integrating this perfectly human trait.

Conclusion

In a complex world, highly sensitive persons bring much-needed empathy, compassion, and balance. Their receptivity to subtle cues and injustices propels them to advocate where others overlook need. Despite criticism or barriers, famous HSP pioneers persisted in pursuing purpose and progress benefiting humanity.

So, fellow sensitive souls, take heart! While sensitivity poses challenges, our innate traits also confer unique gifts if nurtured well. By examining renowned HSPs who leveraged profound talents to change history, we gain the courage to embrace our nature. Their visibility makes space for the 20% wired to experience life uniquely. In standing confidently as sensory superheroes, we transform environments for generations after.

Now, how might highly sensitive people carry such superpowers into the workplace? Does professional success require hiding sensitivity's light under a bushel basket when organizations prize production over people? Or could uniquely compassionate leadership and innovation flow through truly valuing diverse minds and hearts?

Let's explore in the next chapter!

CHAPTER 6

HARNESSING SENSITIVITY IN THE WORKPLACE

My heart pounded as I stared blankly at the conference room whiteboard covered in a dizzying cacophony of multicolored scribbles and arrows. "Synergize deliverables...facilitate metrics..." droned the CEO's booming voice, each word battering my already overloaded senses. Colleagues' expectant gazes bored into me while vertigo threatened as harsh fluorescent lights and the copy machine's relentless whirring drowned out any coherent thoughts. As a Highly Sensitive Person, I knew this stressful workplace environment strained my empathic nervous system beyond capacity. I longed to escape to the serenity of my quiet home and blanket nest, yearning to recover from the endless sensory assault.

At that moment, an epiphany crystallized—why should accomplishing meaningful work rupture the soul of HSPs weathering harsh, depleting workplaces? What strategies enable thriving professionally while honoring sensitivity's contours? If aligned with true callings, perhaps even chaotic conferences would feel less abhorrent?

This chapter explores tailoring careers nurturing humanistic strengths despite domains defined by stoicism. By merging authentic purpose with practical concessions, smoothing sharp reality's edges, let's construct frameworks maximizing passion's flames without burning out!

First, we'll assess how sensitivity shapes ideal vocational trajectories by highlighting critical consciousness warnings when environments collapse through ignorance of innate temperaments requiring customized conditions. Not all flowers bloom pressed inside conformity's beds!

Next, we'll gather wisdom on aligning values with professional paths through insightful exercises eliciting your unique genius, spurring creative entrepreneurial possibilities. Because meaning matters more than money from mindless machinations misaligned with spirit. Holistic well-being outshines wealth earned by unwitting betrayal of self.

Finally, healthy communication techniques and vigilant boundaries foster collaborative camaraderie, preventing depletion by cultural demands disregarding fundamental human needs like downtime beyond ceaseless productivity. If environments cannot nurture sensitivity, sensitively attuned changemakers create the necessary transformation.

a. The impact of sensitivity on career choices and work environments

High sensitivity is much more than just heightened emotional reactions or avoiding loud noises. It encompasses a range of traits and characteristics that can deeply impact how highly sensitive people (HSPs) navigate life and work. An estimated 15-20% of people have sensitive nervous systems that process stimuli more thoroughly. This includes noticing more details, making deeper connections, and experiencing stronger responses to everything from criticism to artwork.

While the depth of processing primes sensitive people to excel creatively and interpersonally, finding fulfilling work aligned with their unique rhythm and temperament remains essential for well-being. Otherwise, overstimulation threatens to compromise their potential.

Elaine Aron, the pioneer researcher on high sensitivity, discovered that 70% of highly sensitive people change careers at least once, frequently because original paths proved either uninspiring or overwhelming. The impact of sensitivity on career choices cannot be minimized if HSPs wish to thrive professionally long-term.

Tuning into Sensitivity's Contours

Embarking on self-discovery around sensitivity's influence on ideal vocational paths begins by first turning inward, reflecting on your distinctive challenges and gifts displayed since childhood.

- Did loud, chaotic school playgrounds at recess force early retreats towards comforting libraries? What creative passion projects or heroic imaginary worlds occupied solo hours? How did sensory details, unseen by peers, captivate your artistic eye? When did empathy's swell for marginalized individuals compel involvement in advocating justice despite social risks?

Noticing early patterns, preferences, and talents reveals critical clues for aligning careers and nurturing your authentic spirit rather than crushing it. Unfortunately, many HSPs wander years vox null waiting for external validation before honoring internal compasses steering towards purpose all along.

Assessing Environmental Factors

Beyond introspection, cataloging previous jobs' highlights and headaches spotlights which elements facilitate peak performance versus those depleting your precious energy.

For instance, perhaps noisy open office floor plans repeatedly sabotaged your productivity and mental clarity despite enjoying the actual work. Or maybe you adored counseling clients yet dreaded paperwork burying you afterward.

Pinpoint precisely which environmental components are frustrated, then reimagine customizing future positions to secure sensitivity-supporting conditions promoting sustainability. Catalog comforts like:

- Flexible remote work options
- Control over physical office settings
- Limiting disruptions
- Options to avoid fluorescent lighting or strong scents
- Freedom wearing noise-canceling headphones when needed
- Autonomy of self-regulating stimulation levels

Mapping Overstimulation Landmines

While assessing past career ups and downs, also document sensitivity-related experiences compromising your wellness, like wrestling with anxiety, depression, or health issues. Especially take notes around overwhelm or exhaustion triggers causing breakdowns.

For instance, maybe unrelenting office politics summoned panic attacks daily. Or perhaps persistent perfectionism demands culminated in burnout and everyday migraines.

These represent landmines inflicting pain whenever you unconsciously tread too near their buried locations again. Pinpoint overstimulation triggers, then consciously avoid positions detonating similar distress moving forward. Not facing the same direction does not indicate failure but rather wisdom. Realizing when environmental fit needs adjusting so your gifts fully shine benefits all.

Cultivating Work Aligned with Your Nature

Of course, most employment involves occasional stressors—the key becomes selecting careers playing to sensitivity's inherent strengths whilst minimizing triggers predictably leading to unhealthy overwhelm.

For highly sensitive people specifically, Dr. Aron recommends careers cultivating their compassionate, conscientious, and creative essence rather than suppressing it through conformity demands. Areas like:

- Counseling, clinical psychology, social work - utilizing emotional attunement to help others
- Creative fields allowing self-expression - visual arts, performing arts, writing, etc.
- Innovation development consultation capitalizing on divergent thinking - design, vision cultivation, Imagineering
- Entrepreneurship crafting self-directed brainchild visions
- Research requiring thorough analysis noticing subtleties - investigation, medicine, systems improvement strategy

The unifying thread remains to pursue meaning through thoughtful integrity. For highly sensitive people, living purposefully guides greater joy than status or wealth alone ever could. Align values with vocational environments supporting sensitive systems, then witness motivation and economic stability, which organically flow.

Work Environments that Align with Sensitivity Strengths

While assessing past employment pinpoints over stimulating factors depleting highly sensitive people, concurrently cataloging environments nurturing productivity spotlights ideal workplace elements to secure future roles proactively.

Beyond physical comforts like subdued lighting or scent-free spaces, sensitivity-supporting cultures demonstrate equal investment in people as productivity. Below are key components providing refuge for sensitive systems to thrive:

Autonomy

Self-determination ranks essential for HSPs managing fluctuating energy, deep focus needs, and emotiveness. Environments granting flexibility around scheduling self-directed workflow prevent overtaxing sensitive nervous systems, acclimating less to a rigid structure.

Whether freelance flexibility or corporate remote work policies, research shows perceived autonomy dramatically improves job satisfaction and performance for highly sensitive people, especially those seeking roles that allow self-governance.

When interviewing, ask questions like:

"How much flexibility exists in customizing schedules around fluctuating energy levels?"

"What remote work opportunities exist for times one absolutely needs pressure-free peace focusing?"

If unsatisfactory responses surface, keep searching for options honoring sensitivity's occasionally unspeakable necessity. The right fit awaits permission, being your true self.

Empathetic Leadership

Highly sensitive people thrive under compassionate leadership, understanding that different working styles all contribute to equal value. Seek executives modeling secure attachment themselves through consistent emotional availability, direct communication, and transparency regarding expectations.

In interviews, ask:

"How do you support introverted or highly perceptive team members?"

"What communication channels exist clarifying questions instantly to prevent unhelpful conjecture or anxiety?"

Take note whether leaders cast people-pleasing, small-talk preferences as company culture cornerstones—sensitivity requires space diverging certain ingrained rituals without shame. Opt instead for executive teams honoring humanity's colorful diversity beyond conformity.

Healthy Collegial Relations

Toxic work cultures threaten sensitivity's sustainability long-term despite loving the actual vocation. Highly sensitive people absorb surrounding emotional fields profoundly. Where trust and goodwill are lacking, anxiety inevitably snowballs, sabotaging once harmonious teams.

When researching potential employers, notice during interviews whether staff mill congenially around offices or rarely acknowledge each other. Do leaders reference supporting employees' holistic well-being or primarily praise sacrificial dedication?

Seeking healthy work relations safeguards sensitivity. Our gifts bloom, benefiting all when honored, not exploited. We drive humanity forward, dwelling in habitats built for egalitarian thriving. For highly sensitive people, especially, supportive company cultures grant freedom fully shining.

Quiet Spaces for Reflection

Noise constantly commands highly sensitive people's attention unless preventing such infringement. Environments failing to restrict endless disruptions rarely retain their most creative assets as long as genius flows richest in stillness.

If your potential employers lack basic soundproofing or solo workstations allowing insulation from open office chatter, keep seeking. Leaders invested in people provide infrastructure mitigating overstimulation.

Ask questions like:

"What quiet spaces exist onsite should one need concentration recovering from offsite conferences or collaborations?"

"How do teams prevent or minimize sudden schedule changes upending planning routines so important for conscientious people?"

Thoughtful accommodations demonstrate an understanding of neurodiversity's common challenges. You deserve executive teams embracing sensitivity's occasional necessity to retreat when delicately overwhelmed. We all win through compassion.

Personal Interests and Professional Aspirations

High sensitivity's double-edged sword equally proved a blessing and curse before awareness transformed perspective. My vivid imagination conjured rich inner worlds, yet loud external reality often stifled its expression. Fearing judgment, I hid my heart's poetry from rude glares—until one attuned mentor saw gifts that others deemed gaffes. "Your perceptive nervous system is an instrument requiring tuning so beauty plays freely again," she whispered. "All parts create harmony."

She suggested directing emotional sensitivity towards written expression—poetry felt too personal, so I journaled instead, processing life's nuance. Soon, a teacher noticed my assignments demonstrated empathy and wisdom unusual for someone so young. "Your writing holds old soul. Have you considered counseling highly sensitive people?" he asked. Suddenly, clarity dawned on fulfillment's path already laid through past pains, granting vision to lift other struggling spirits. I enrolled immediately in peer counseling trauma survivors. Everyone healed—including me.

What initially seemed sensitivity's sabotage transformed into professional purpose through another's grace, noticing potential I still hid from myself. Highly sensitive people must remember looking inward reveals only shadows of unexpressed talents still awaiting outer manifestation. Our mentors shine light, so we also lead others out of darkness through creativity's unconventional redemption. Sensitivity strengthens relating when structured, supporting courage and outweighing old fears of dreaming differently.

Trusted advisors see sensitive people's possibilities, waiting patiently for potential's awakening. They understand highly responsive nervous systems wrestling challenges when force-fed conformity's relentless demands. Like oxygen to a fire, sensitivity grows when given room, becoming the warmth one secretly sought their whole life.

What mentors illuminated your professional journey? How did their wisdom provide clarity, community, or confidence in unveiling purpose? Seek those attuned counselors speaking sensitivity's language—through compassion, you'll discover the creative call that was yours all along.

Challenges HSPs May Face in Various Careers

Despite best efforts to prevent conditions overwhelming highly sensitive people at work, balancing vocational skill development and safeguarding delicate nervous systems often proves challenging for even the most conscious HSPs and supportive leaders.

Recognizing common workplace struggles sensitivity poses for those wired deeply interpersonally and perceptually allows proactively strengthening self-care skills to persevere and thrive when heatmap headaches hit. Here are key hotspots spurring occupational overwhelm, especially for HSPs:

People-Pleasing Pressure

Hardwired empaths habitually morph like chameleons, adopting the predominant emotional hue in any environment. So highly sensitive people frequently camouflage instinctively, masking true feelings or preferences, keeping relationships peaceful—even at personal health's expense.

Yet suppressing authentic needs breeds silent resentment once depleted energy resources require replenishment. When professionally placating others regularly despite internally screaming, tap brakes, assessing whether the current vocational path aligns values, gifts, and workload bandwidth. If imbalance persists, dare boldly dream of career priorities that nurture your sensitive spirit. The world deserves your whole, healthy self.

Overfunctioning

Highly sensitive people naturally notice unfilled needs, and compassion compels them to fill voids. You rescue the team, picking up the slack when someone leaves unexpectedly—volunteer steering committees lacking strong visionary direction. Your workplace benefits stay busy for six months, providing unpaid maternity leave coverage so nothing slips. Does this sound familiar?

Hyperresponsible HSPs frequently overfunction, believing whole systems crumble unless they personally ensure optimal operations constantly. But playing Atlas and bearing workplace weight on your shoulders alone invites fatigue, not sustainable functioning. Overfunctioning often indicates inequitably distributed labor—even divvying some load lightens your legs so all walk farther together. Speak up against redistributing unreasonable expectations on you. Everyone wins through compassionate courage leading change.

People Management

Direct reports represent highly sensitive managers' Achilles heels—navigating personality changes inevitably brings interpersonal challenges. Sensitive souls struggle to uphold organizational priorities when opposing employees' fundamental welfare and psychological health. Imposing unpleasant mandates feels tyrannical, forcing square pegs to smoosh round holes. People-focused leaders require healthy boundaries, preventing rescue attempts and thwarting growth needed to emerge through necessary conflicts. Otherwise, saving teams from critical lessons invites stifled innovation and passive aggression that fester unaddressed. Lead through listening, then leverage insight, cultivating cultural change that benefits all. And when structures still stifle souls, dare topple the status quo built by gone generations lacking modern consciousness. The future beckons your revolution.

Toxic Work Cultures

Highly sensitive people thrive in healthy company cultures, nurturing staff with open communication, collaborative workflows, constructive feedback, and encouraging growth. Environments characterized by secrecy, competition, cattiness, or criticism often repel emotionally attuned workers eventually despite compelling vocational mission pull. Why? Because sensitivity requires feeling safe, being vulnerable, developing strengths, and revealing limitations needing support. Psychologically unsafe websites signal employees to hide their truth and real selves to survive, not thrive together. Quitting toxic teams to preserve well-being proves warranted despite financial risks when authenticity suffocates beneath brokenness. Wounded people sometimes search for outer success, burying inner worlds that require healing. But BandAids cannot mend mortal wounds—those penetrate the soul needing wisdom's touch. When cultural rot sickens foundations, sensitive people abandon ships preserving sanity, then build healthier communities elsewhere.

Insensitivity Regarding Sensitivity

Although neurodiversity awareness grows—recognizing conditions like ADHD or autism spectrums requires customized support—high sensitivity still flies under the workplace radar. Without proper discrimination protections, HSPs endure dismissal, gaslighting, or punishment when neurological traits like extra stimulation sensitivity or processing time require reasonable accommodations. Often, abandonment results in feeling too different withstanding daily exclusion anxiety or demands exhausting the very essence spirit chose to enter earth. Clarity sheds light on blindness though—what judges often misunderstand, compassion makes whole. So sensitive beings must grow skins thick enough, weathering ignorance yet permeable, receiving nourishment source feeding dreams, for when we empower ourselves first, filters clarifying society's muddy waters emerge next. Leadership shines brightest from life's very margins inwardly freed. Consider limitations and gifts when given permission to fully shape life's canvas. The margins await their rightful center stage.

In summary, high sensitivity's double-edged blade cuts sharp, initially wrestling self-doubt before transforming perspective, revealing uncommon gifts. By recognizing environmental factors supporting versus suppressing productivity and consciously designing careers aligning sensitivity's strengths, highly sensitive people flourish professionally as intended. When leaders nurture their compassionate, conscientious colleagues through accommodation and inclusive education, unique talents transform entire workplaces for everyone's benefit.

The future beckons your sensitive strengths—shall we answer its call together?

b. Strategies for success, including finding fulfilling careers and entrepreneurial pursuits

As highly sensitive people, finding fulfillment and success in our careers is vitally important, yet it can also be uniquely challenging. Our sensitive nervous systems thrive when we feel purpose and passion in our work but may become easily overwhelmed by overstimulating or unsupportive environments. By understanding our specialized needs as HSPs and seeking the right career fit, we can channel our gifts to make an impact while maintaining our well-being.

In this section, we will explore strategies highly sensitive people can employ to achieve career and entrepreneurial success without sacrifice.

First, we will discuss the power of alignment in matching our innate strengths and values to suitable professions. Next, we will examine factors to weigh when deciding between career paths and life balance. Further, we will overview research on mindfulness practices that can aid workplace performance. Finally, we will suggest specific career fields and self-employment avenues ideal for sensitive individuals to consider.

By taking an intentional approach tailored to our unique wiring, we can find professional avenues through which our compassion, conscientiousness, and creativity blossom. Our success need not come at the cost of overwhelm when we instead view our sensitivity as the gift it is.

The Power of Alignment

It's critical that we find work that aligns with our values, passions, and innate strengths. When our work resonates at a core level, we unlock our potential for both fulfillment and success.

I learned this lesson the hard way in my mid-20s when I pursued a lucrative job in investment banking. On paper, it seemed like a smart move—the salary allowed me a comfortable lifestyle, and the fast-paced environment kept boredom at bay. However, I felt empty and dissatisfied most days, dreading the 80+ hour work-weeks filled with endless meetings, presentations, and office politics. I powered through using sheer will and copious amounts of coffee, flooding my sensitive nervous system with cortisol.

Over time, anxiety and depression crept in, no matter how many yoga classes or nature retreats I squeezed into rare days off. A vague sense that this couldn't be "it" nagged despite societal messages insisting I should feel grateful. And deep down, an inner knowing whispered that my true calling awaited elsewhere.

When debilitating migraines from stress-induced exhaustion forced my hand, I paused to reflect on what really mattered. Surprisingly, money and status ranked low once basic needs were covered. Instead, I yearned to make a difference, even in a small way, to feel inspired and passionate about my day-to-day work, to use my Highly Sensitive Person traits like emotional attunement, creativity, and intuition in service of people and causes igniting my spirit.

In assessing past jobs I enjoyed, themes emerged, revealing ideal work conditions. Flexibility and autonomy featured prominently since rigid schedules easily depleted my sensitive nervous system. As did remote options limiting overstimulation. Most importantly, supporting individuals going through major life transitions lit me up, affirming my calling.

Armed with hard-won clarity, I pivoted into writing and speaking, specializing in personal growth and emotional well-being. My blend of empathetic spirit combined with HSP superpowers like profound listening and encouragement empowers readers undergoing major life transitions. No longer sacrificing myself chasing money or security, fulfillment now energizes my work.

The takeaway? Highly sensitive people thrive when we align work to our true passions and design personalized conditions protecting our sensitive natures. Define what success means for YOU beyond society's limited scope. Get radically honest about ideal environments, allowing your distinctive gifts to shine. Then, take bold, faith-powered steps towards that vision without looking back. Purpose and prosperity await those bold enough to live their soul's true calling.

Choosing the right career path vs well-being

Like many highly sensitive people, I've grappled with the complex interplay between career ambitions and personal well-being. My sensitive system withstands limited stress despite a fierce drive pushing me towards ever-greater goals. Recurrently, I've sacrificed too much striving for the next achievement, forcing my sensitive psyche into overload until illness halted my relentless push upwards.

This pattern crystallized during my corporate executive climb, ruthlessly prioritizing burnout-inducing advancement over self-care and life balance. My sensitive soul whispered caution as vertigo and heart palpitations signaled a nervous system taxed to its limits. But obsessed with the intoxication of "success" and afraid to disrupt forward career momentum, I brushed aside the warning signs until adrenal fatigue, panic attacks, and depression necessitated radical change.

In the painful aftermath, tough questions confronted me. Had chasing lofty career status fulfilled me or masked an emptiness within which no title or salary could satisfy? Did scaling the corporate ladder actually align with my Highly Sensitive Person core—one nourished through meaning, creativity, and purpose rather than power or profit? Had my own disconnect from emotional needs and spiritual values steered me down an unsustainable path?

From those reflections surfaced game-changing personal clarity: while still desiring to make a difference in roles utilizing my fullest gifts, no external accomplishment merits compromising health or denying my sensitive essence, requiring ample rest, inspiration, and heart-centered connection.

So, I consciously redesigned my work to align with HSP wellness needs. Today, as an author and speaker, I model sustainable success grounded in radical self-care and emotional attunement. My readers and I craft lives together, allowing ambition to coexist with humanity by honoring sensitivity's rhythms. Together, we fuse purpose with peace.

The path toward fulfillment rarely follows a straight line but winds, dips, and curves in unexpected ways. Careers form but one thread of life's intricate tapestry. By holding our journey lightly yet learning from each twist along the way, we sensitive souls glean wisdom guiding us into deeper alignment with our best selves—our greatest success.

Mindfulness at workplace

As a profoundly perceptive Highly Sensitive Person, I've wrestled with feeling overwhelmed by workplace sensory input—relentless chatter, clacking keyboards, glaring monitors, stale air. In desperation, I'd escape to the bathroom, seeking respite from endless mental chatter, worrying about unfinished projects or conflicts with prickly colleagues. But quick fixes never lasted long before fraying nerves necessitated another break.

Until discovering mindfulness. By training my brain to stay calmly rooted in the present no matter the surrounding stimuli, sensory explosions suddenly subsided to manageable levels through heightened conscious awareness alone. Emerging research confirmed what I experienced firsthand—mindfulness rewires neural pathways, reducing reactivity.

Mindfulness practices teach the sensitive brain to consciously wrangle wandering attention toward immediate sensory experiences using tactical, mental cues. For example, during stressful meetings, I discreetly tap one fingertip, silently focusing on physical sensations in that spot. Simply feeling subtle skin contact grounds cognitive circuits otherwise fixating on confrontational discourse or imagined negative outcomes. Like a mental lifeline, this discreet physical anchor retrieves my frazzled thoughts from toxic mental eddies swirling dark imaginings about worst-case scenarios. Soon, calm rationality returns, empowering clear communications.

Beyond centering cognitive flexibility, mindfulness also unlocks relational gifts leveraging sensitivity's strengths. By consciously deepening felt connections with colleagues through compassionate attunement, even difficult personalities morph into potential teachers, revealing behavioral insights and hidden emotional wounds, spurring unnecessary provocations. This mindful lens elucidates universal struggles binding humanity. Suddenly, sensitivity becomes profound strength, sensitizing us to scarce resources for healing community divisions—empathy, courage, and love.

Thus, mindfulness frees highly sensitive people for leadership reluctantly shouldered yet urgently required. No longer overwhelmed by circumstances seemingly beyond control, presence grounds intuitive inner vision while clarifying external actions manifesting positive change. Highly sensitive people may enter reluctantly but mindfully lead powerfully by transforming environments through radical vulnerability and compassion.

Best Career

Seeking my ideal career path as a Highly Sensitive Person long felt like chasing a phantom, always remaining two steps ahead yet barely visible. Early traditional pursuits led down ambivalent avenues, leaving me empty and unsatisfied despite outward measures of success. But still, certainty eluded me.

Gradually, wisdom awoke, realizing fulfilling work for sensitive types arises from courageously questioning cultural constructs of achievement and social status. We uncover callings hidden in plain sight by casting off constraining conventional templates. My own sensitivity contains built-in GPS revealing direction through negative space—where lack of passion signals misalignment. Subtract obligations draining precious energy. What possibilities spark inspiration enduring beyond initial novelty?

A spark of joy lights up my spirit whenever I can support others and help them find clarity—I feel drawn to caring roles that allow compassionate listening and encouragement.

Yet tackling individuals' heavy emotional burdens full-time risked energetic over-load. Teaching offered solutions combining working alone preparing lessons and then engaging directly uplifting students. Academia allows the pursuit of abiding interests through research and sharing insights, furthering human understanding. Writing brought self-expression and service.

Still, financial considerations necessitated balance. Consulting and utilizing ana-lytical expertise made self-employment feasible finally. Remote flexibility stabilized sensitive nervous systems vulnerable to overstimulation. Ongoing attunement fine-tunes optimal alignment as interests evolve across the years. Yet career con-tentment remains, recognizing labeled success matters less than daily purpose and passion.

Highly sensitive people thrive when work elicits individual talents, makes mean-ing by aiding others, and aligns values with the organization's purpose. Seek environments allowing sensitivity to enhance, not hinder, performance through acknowledging unique needs. Build schedules supporting productivity absent depletion. Request accommodations if unavailable—frame requiring quiet spaces and remote options as boosting workplace effectiveness since sensitive people accomplish exponentially more in suitable habitats. Consider freelancing or care-fully evaluated entrepreneurism. But attend first to inner wisdom nudging your special gifts towards destinies fulfilling beyond the wildest imagination. Awaiting adventures surpass limited beliefs. Your life's calling patiently beckons. Shall we begin? Destiny awaits!

Self-Employment

Despite sensitivity's challenges, we highly perceptive beings also possess mighty visionary powers—keen emotional radar detecting scarce resources, healing unspoken hurts, plus heightened creativity birthing innovations transforming stuck mindsets. These potent gifts demand full expression, revolutionizing systems and policies benefiting humanity and our shared world. Behold profound callings awaiting sensitive change-makers!

Yet pursuing world-changing careers within traditional workplace constraints often requires energy-draining adaptations that dim sensitivity's light. Corporate cultures typically prize productivity over people, ignoring designers needing conditions protecting fragile nervous systems bombarded by endless stimuli noise. Self-employment's flexibility offers solutions reconciling ambitious visions with highly sensitive natures through curating customized habitats nurturing peak performance absent depletion.

If entrepreneurship elicits excitement rather than exhaustion, carefully consider potent gifts suggesting ideal market offerings. What injustice perturbed your soul until soothed only by addressing its root causes? What whispers rouse your sleeping passions nightly as your soul tugs your heart towards actualizing fully alive? Mine these musings for directional gold. Discover abilities that make your spirit sing and the world brighter, then build offering channels gifting these to the public eagerly awaiting your distinctive solutions.

Still, self-employment necessitates more than splashy ideas—successful execution requires strategic planning and consistent, determined effort. Assess personal readiness honestly—are you willing to postpone gratification for future gains? Comfortable with uncertainty awaiting stable income? Skilled managing time given flexibility's temptation towards distraction? Disciplined when accountability depends upon self rather than supervisors? If not now, cultivate abilities aligned with entrepreneurial demands through classes or job experiences educating needed expertise. Waiting for perfect timing usually signals fear avoidance rather than prudent preparation.

Despite challenges, self-employment frees sensitive selves for bold living on purpose. Shed confining corporate constraints; get comfortable coloring outside conformity lines. No more contorting sensitive square-pegs muffing sparkly edges squeezing into dull round drudgery holes depleting soulful essence. Let your distinctiveness shine, attracting tribes who finally "get" you. Build worlds where you belong by becoming the change you wish to see. The future beckons your innovative solutions birthed by aligned sensitive natures crafted for a wider world awaiting your unconventional wisdom.

Shall we get started?

c.   Workplace challenges and solutions for HSPs

Amid frenzied modern workplaces, sensitivity's gifts often wilt, overwhelmed by noisy interactions. Yet with compassion and inclusion, minor accommodations smooth communication channels, unlocking relationship-building talents benefiting all. By reframing tendencies as strengths, not weaknesses, then bridging understanding through anonymity and check-ins, teams leverage highly perceptive professionals' innate skills, uplifting environments towards greater humanity.

Communication and Collaboration

As deeply caring and conscientious employees, highly sensitive people (HSPs) excel at collaboration when communication norms align with their needs. However, traditional workplace interactions often prove draining.

Luckily, minor accommodations smoothing collaboration channels can unlock HSPs' relationship-building talents, benefiting all. For example, brainstorming sessions prime creativity when including focused solo reflection beforehand, allowing introverted processing and promoting equitable idea sharing. Regular feedback forms distributed anonymously prevent HSPs from overreacting to personalized criticism. Weekly individual check-ins foster closer understanding between colleagues while preventing unnecessary interruptions derailing deep work.

Most importantly, transparently educate peers on sensitivity, framing it positively as a workplace asset. Debunk misconceptions that "requiring" occasional solitude means isolation or superiority. Share how self-knowledge of one's rhythms and sensory needs prevents depletion, enabling better service to the team overall. Soon, HSP superpowers shine.

Stress Management and Burnout Prevention

Highly sensitive people possess incredible plate-spinning abilities, keeping numerous essential workplace elements smoothly flowing. However, such intense attentiveness risks missing personal overload signals before crashing. Establishing healthy frontline defenses proves critical.

Begin by identifying initial overwhelm signs like shortness, impatience, or foggy thinking hindering concentration. Next, make a list of go-to self-care remedies for soothing frazzled nerves, perhaps brief meditation breaks, herbal tea, quiet walks, or inspirational reading. To strengthen resilience long-term, adopt lifestyle buffers like ample sleep, smart device downtime, calming transit choices, and early help solicitation—psychotherapy fortifies sensitive systems wonderfully!

Finally, limit workplace martyr mentalities insisting on completing every last daily task even when depleted. Better resting fully tomorrow than soldiering on joylessly. Frame valuing personal health needs as necessary ethics benefiting all. When HSPs model sustainability, self-care penetrates organizational culture exponentially!

Setting Boundaries: Balancing Work and Personal Needs

Navigating work-life balance as highly sensitive people involves transcending fears around upholding personal boundaries. Conditioning to avoid "rocking boats" challenges directly stating workflow preferences or calling quits when energy wanes. However, authentic limits foster daily functioning, protecting sensitive systems from depletion damage.

Begin practicing boundary-setting gently refusing non-urgent administrative tasks or pointless meetings when focused projects require attention. If initially uncomfortable, scripts help strengthen confidence until saying "no" feels as natural as breathing. Example: "I'm happy assisting long-term, yet today's schedule remains full. Let's reconnect when bandwidth frees up!" Feeling guilty means you've given away too much power—take it back graciously.

Additionally, set work duration limits stopping at reasonable hours. Unless occasional crunch deadlines require all-hands-on-deck commitment, consistently clocking out prevents burnout. Managers invested in people understand varying mental needs; if yours disrespect sensitivity's contours, perhaps environments exist elsewhere nurturing your gifts better. Either way, uphold work-life harmony through boundaries as strong as stone, declaring, "My well-being holds priority before any professional demands!" Then, watch creativity really unfold.

Conclusion

Thriving as highly sensitive working professionals involves embracing sensitivity's paradox - heightened awareness equally curses and blesses. By courageously championing workplace conditions optimized for HSP gifts like deep creativity, insight, and conscientiousness, we model humanistic standards benefitting all personality types. May empowering mindsets uplift new perspectives on neurological diversity's necessity. Our distinctive offerings await fuller expression—onwards together!

Now having covered aligning sensitive strengths with ideal vocational environments, fulfilling time remains exploring self-care strategies preventing depletion as passion's waves inevitably crest then crash when dancing to daily life's rhythms. Please journey with me into Chapter 7 - Building Resilience and Coping Skills for sensitive systems weathering inevitable overwhelm spells with newfound wisdom and grace...

CHAPTER 7

BUILDING RESILIENCE AND COPING SKILLS

I watched the storm rage outside my window, the wind whipping the trees violently as rain pounded the glass in heavy sheets. Flashes of lightning illuminated the dark skies, followed by booming cracks of thunder. I wrapped a soft blanket around myself, feeling unsettled by the turbulence.

My mind drifted back to Chapter 3, where we first discussed creating personal "safe zones", those calm spaces that provide sanctuary when feeling emotionally overwhelmed. I glanced around my quiet living room, candles glowing softly, and breathed a sigh of relief. At least I had a refuge while the storm passed.

Yet I know that when sensitivity's storms stretch on interminably, even my safe zone cannot shield me forever. Emotional resilience wavers for even the most self-aware HSP during trying times. We all endure seasons that test our coping capacities.

How can we weather turbulent emotional storms without losing hope or strength? This chapter gathers insights on building lifelong resilience and mental muscle to bend while battered, not break. We'll explore stress management techniques and mindfulness practices specially designed for the highly sensitive system. You'll uncover the vital importance of self-care in preventing depletion and affirm the power of gentle assertiveness training.

My goal is that by the chapter's end, you step out and survey life's messy landscape with fresh eyes - perhaps noticing new possibilities budding where storms once loomed ominously. There are gifts seeded in the darkness, often revealed by lightning's flash.

Onwards we go, towards morning's light!

a. Techniques for emotional resilience and stress management

As highly sensitive people, our deeply felt emotions and heightened sensitivity can make life feel like a constant rollercoaster. Small frustrations feel big, criticism cuts deep, and the busy modern world often overwhelms our delicate nervous systems. Yet, while sensitivity brings rich blessings, to fully thrive requires cultivating inner resilience to weather inevitable storms.

The good news?

Resilience can grow over time as we gently tend the garden of our spirit. Like building muscular strength through gradual training, emotional resilience strengthens as we employ targeted practices meeting sensitivity's specialized needs. By understanding our extra receptivity as an innate trait requiring customized care—not a personal shortcoming—we rewrite limiting stories sabotaging our potential. From this compassionate insight blossoms the motivation to nurture ourselves with wisdom and patience.

Let's gather time-tested techniques explicitly designed to bolster a Highly Sensitive Person's resilience, equipping us to ride out life's challenges with our sensitive nature intact. Consider incorporating these supportive life habits into your days - not all at once, but steadily and sustainably. Adjust approaches fitting your lifestyle and energy levels at this moment. Over time, as emotional muscles strengthen, what once seemed impossible journeys become second nature. Soon, you'll lift your eyes from the path stumbled upon to behold newfound vistas awakened within.

Nurturing Inner Calm Through Mindfulness

Where raging rivers once threatened drowning sensitive systems, mindfulness' tranquil waters flow. This ancient practice trains awareness, dwelling consciously in each passing moment without clinging or judgment when thoughts wander astray. Over time, mental muscles strengthen, enabling highly sensitive people to observe even unpleasant emotions with non-reactive grace, thus preventing distress from escalating through obsessive overanalysis typical for our busy minds.

Mindfulness is the art of conscious living, fully present, inhabiting your days beyond past regrets or future worries—simply feeling, tasting, and sensing each shift in experience without analysis. Attempting this remains challenging initially, as sensitive beings default to interpreting life narratively through emotions' metaphorical lens. But dedicating just minutes daily to focusing senses upon immediate surroundings peacefully realigns perspective from anxiety's stories stressfully projected ahead.

Sitting here feeling the earth underneath me, the sunlight warming my skin, my beloved dog snuggled up offering affection—I'm struck by the simple perfection of this moment. The beauty of mindfulness shines through, helping me notice small miracles that I often miss when hurriedly chasing obligations that leave me unfulfilled. I take a deep breath and immerse myself in the sanctuary of the present. I try not to let worries steal this preciousness away. The solidity of the ground beneath my feet calms me, stilling the storms once swirling through my mind. Through mindfulness, I find stillness that settles my spirit. Staying focused on the simplicity and beauty of this very instant brings a sense of gentle calm within reach.

Cultivating Self-Care to Prevent Burnout

Sensitive beings easily pour from generously filled cups when nourishing self-care habits sustain our giving spirits. Yet busy modernity often erodes life margins until finding emotional resilience requires reclaiming time and refueling depleted inner reservoirs. By consciously implementing restorative practices into daily routines, highly sensitive people prevent the slow slide toward burnout from simmering unacknowledged upon backburners.

Begin practicing self-love by simply noticing your own highest good as a priority, equaling commitment to showing up for others. What refills your cup today— soaking feet after a tiring workweek, a long nature walk's restorative rhythms, catching up with cherished friends, or curling up on cushions with favorite music, scented candle, and uplifting book? Gather beloved treasures feeding your sensitive soul, then unapologetically indulge in this sensitivity-centric care, for in receiving joy yourself, you'll spread smiles further.

Highly sensitive people also require budgeting downtime after social gatherings or stimulating input. Monitor energy levels by noticing when irritation signals overextension. At first, fatigue flickers subtly and easily dismissed, plowing stubbornly onwards. Yet cascading consequences amplify if disregarding escalating tension headaches, fuzzy concentration, and emotional reactivity. Prevent total overwhelm by scheduling breaks between demanding cognitive projects or people-filled events. Collapse becomes less inevitable once you balance productivity with intentional rejuvenation.

You deserve to feel wholly resourced. Embrace self-care not as a luxury but as a cornerstone of foundations upholding highly sensitive health. Life's color dulls when constantly depleted brightens, resting in sensitivity's customized care. Therefore, love yourself well—you'll shine blessings.

Establishing Healthy Interpersonal Boundaries

Highly sensitive people naturally attune profoundly to surrounding emotional energies often absorbing others' moods into their auras until frequently indistinguishable, where foreign anxiety stops and authentic feelings start. To sustain healthy relationships without losing inner integrity requires implementing firm interpersonal boundaries that compassionately honor your needs.

For instance, sensitive people-pleasers habitually accommodate unreasonable requests despite resentment brewing beneath surface smiles. We ignore obvious exhaustion serving guests' endless needs or answering late-night crisis calls from draining friends. But behind flimsy façades allowing mistreatment, the heart's true yearnings ache, longing for respectfully reciprocated care.

Begin gently training loved ones through open communication—"Susan, I care deeply but cannot drive you to midnight airport runs when working early tomorrow. Let's brainstorm backup options preserving all wellbeing." With compassionate honesty, clearly assert your emotional limits without aggression. If met with criticism for establishing self-care priorities, perhaps reassess whether toxicity now outweighs meaningful relating. You deserve to shine bright.

Additionally, visualize an energy shield surrounding the body, providing metaphysical insulation near manipulative personalities. Picture or describe protective spheres aloud, maintaining healthy space when situationally unable to exit conversations temporarily. Highly sensitive people require fortifying personal cocoons against psychic vampires who cannot see beyond self-serving agendas. Yet also send compassion towards these emotionally underdeveloped beings equally deserving happiness through awakening from deluded selfishness someday. For now, you model enlightened relating—delicately sidestepping fangs by upholding healthy boundaries with wisdom and grace.

In conclusion, highly sensitive people gain tools to thrive despite modern life's insensitive velocity with compassionate self-understanding, targeted resilience practices, and firm yet flexible interpersonal boundaries. Gradually implement mindfulness, ample self-care, and energy protection skills, steadying emotional equilibrium once easily capsized by demanding drain. Soon, your distinctive gifts emerge unhindered by old stories of inadequacy, unleashing sensitive ingenuity upon the world. In unlocking inner wells, resilience fortifies exterior impacts, becoming simply water rolling off a self-aware duck's back. Where storms once bowed fragile reeds now stands a strong-rooted oak. You always possessed such resilient beauty, which is now fully seen.

b. Mindfulness exercises and relaxation techniques tailored for HSPs

As highly sensitive people, our extra-receptive nervous systems often struggle to balance the richness of life's beauty alongside its intensity. From sensory overload to emotional flooding, overwhelm lurks as our companion. Yet ancient wisdom reminds us that peace lies not in changing outer chaos but in transforming inner response. Through mindfulness, we train awareness, meeting each moment with a non-judgmental presence. Over time, it replaces reactivity with an expanded perspective, gently upholding equilibrium no matter the circumstance.

Mindfulness means consciously inhabiting this instant, neither clinging to the past nor projecting imagined futures. We anchor in direct experience, noticing thoughts and sensations without blocking or forcing. Imagine thoughts as leaves drifting downstream, simply witnessing their presence and letting them float by. Return attention gently to the breath, bodily felt sense, or sounds nearby when the mind wanders. Non-striving, non-grasping, just pure observing.

At first, maintaining a mindful presence challenges even seasoned meditators; the brain instinctively fixates on analyzing, planning, and worrying. But mindfulness teachers respond, not reacting. We acknowledge the willful shift of focus to the present, not trying to control anything. With compassionate persistence, the monkey mind settles into stillness. From expanded awareness, we respond consciously, engaging life with a refreshed presence.

The Benefits of Mindful Awareness Practices

Why engage in mindfulness? Beyond calming benefits during practice, mindfulness promotes resilience in managing daily stressors. Research shows dedicated meditators concentrate better, empathize profoundly, and regulate emotions adaptively. MRI scans confirm seasoned practitioners activate self-soothing brain regions intuitively. Other studies correlate mindfulness strength to reduced depression, anxiety, and pain sensitivity. By repeatedly redirecting attention to the richness of now with non-reactivity, we quite literally rewire neural pathways to exude less stress while radiating more presence.

A common mindfulness myth believes eliminating all thought comprises success. But inner chatter continues; we simply relate differently—picture thoughts as clouds drifting by rather than storms in which you're immersed. You have choices—either obsessively analyzing each cloud trying to control the sky or peacefully observing transience, allowing weather patterns their flow. There lies freedom.

Mindfulness practices expose our lack of control amidst swirling chaos. Challenging childhoods and genetic predispositions contribute - but present moments sculpt future well-being far more than the past. We mindfully meet whatever arises with clarity, not judgment; turmoil becomes teacher, not tyrant.

Cultivate Beginner's Mind

"In the beginner's mind, there are many possibilities. In the expert's mind, there are few."

Approach mindfulness practices, embodying childlike curiosity, not strained striving. Root into foundations like breath awareness or body scanning without layered expectations. When frustration arises, pause and smile, gently reconnecting to presence. Each moment offers renewed choice.

Progress unfolds slowly and then suddenly through consistent nurturance. But if measuring by imagined milestones, mindfulness becomes another source of self-judgment limiting freedom. Instead, adopt lightness meeting practices sincerely while releasing attachment to outcomes. Trust inner wisdom; simply continue showing up. Transformation secretly unfolds between efforts if we relax into being rather than relentlessly doing. Allow mindfulness its magic.

Calming Practices for Overwhelmed Sensitive Systems

When emotional flooding or physical discomfort builds internally, gentle mindfulness techniques provide solace in rebalancing sensitivity scales during turmoil. Compassionately explore favorite centering support.

The breath always awaits as a faithful anchor when torrents strike—simply feel inhalations and exhalations steadily entering and exiting without controlling the pace. Deep inhales and prolonged exhales signal safety, calming the nervous system quickly.

Body scans promote presence by sequentially isolating attention on regions scanning for sensations. Notice tensions or relaxation, temperature variances, pulsing, or stillness. Accept feedback without criticism; judgment further aggravates distress. Simply breathe into areas eliciting reaction without forcing change. Let be and allow time; it's patient wisdom.

Walking meditation fosters mindful embodiment in motion—a particularly effective grounding when seated stillness exacerbates restlessness—deliberately pace lifting, moving, and placing each foot while tracking physical impressions. Gaze softly downwards to avoid overstimulation if outdoors or gently lift eyes towards the horizon, expanding peripheral vision indoors and promoting tranquil alertness. Embrace simplicity and return steps whenever mental meanderings hijack the journey. Continue amidst setbacks with compassion, not condemnation. Progress lies around the bend once we stop battling the true path.

Consistency cultivating presence prevents persistent overwhelm from accumulating exponentially until hypersensitive nervous systems implode. Through dedicating just minutes daily, meeting the moments arising with mindfulness, not resistance, spaciousness emerges amidst chaos once considered intolerable. We hold all experiences lightly, engaging without clinging or condemning. Developing mindful resilience requires surrender, not striving - effortlessly allowing rather than straining for highly sensitive beings. Relax into your sensitive birthright; liberation lies within.

c. The importance of self-care, setting boundaries and prioritizing Self-Care

As a Highly Sensitive Person (HSP), self-care and setting healthy boundaries are essential for managing overwhelm and thriving. Due to our deeply feeling natures, we tend to deplete our energy reserves faster than others. Without proper self-care, we risk burning out emotionally, mentally, and physically.

Likewise, boundaries help us conserve energy by determining what we will and won't accept in our lives. They allow us to filter out unnecessary stressors and harmful situations. Mastering self-care and boundary setting are pivotal skills on the HSP journey.

Defining Self-Care

Self-care refers to the daily practices and behaviors we engage in to nurture our health and well-being. For HSPs, self-care looks like:

- Getting adequate sleep
- Eating a balanced, nutritious diet
- Exercising and moving our bodies
- Taking time to relax and recharge
- Engaging in hobbies and activities, we enjoy
- Spending time in nature and peaceful environments
- Practicing mindfulness, meditation, or breathwork
- Keeping a therapy or support system
- Setting aside regular solo time
- Avoiding overstimulating situations when needed

We all have basic self-care needs. But as HSPs, we require extra TLC, given our heightened sensitivity. Self-care is not merely about bubble baths and treats. It means skillfully attending to our bodies and souls—our inner ecosystems. When our self-care routine falters, we risk plunging into physical and emotional chaos.

Mastering The Art of Boundary Setting

Boundaries determine what we allow into our lives and what we filter out to protect our energy. As HSPs, poor boundaries drain us severely. We unwittingly take on other people's problems and emotions due to our immense empathy. Creating firm yet flexible boundaries prevents us from overextending as highly sensitive beings.

Examples of HSP boundaries include:

- Asserting your need for alone time
- Saying "no" to events or commitments that overwhelm you
- Asking for accommodations at work to manage stimulation
- Leaving situations where others disrespect you
- Limiting time with drama-prone or manipulative individuals -Setting technology usage rules to prevent overstimulation
- Tuning out upsetting news coverage when needed

Remember—boundaries work both ways. While enforcing our own limits, we must also respect the boundaries of others. Effective boundary setting improves our relationships and daily functioning.

Overcoming Obstacles to Self-Care Through Self-Understanding

Given our highly empathetic natures, self-care can be challenging. We often put others' needs before our own. However, neglecting self-care inevitably hurts our loved ones as we grow resentful and depleted. Other obstacles include:

- Feeling guilty for taking personal time
- Lacking awareness of our sensory needs
- Struggling to identify and communicate our boundaries

- Fearing conflict, judgment, or rejection from enforcing boundaries

Yet, with self-understanding, we can reframe these perceived obstacles. We recognize that self-care makes us better partners, parents, friends, and conscientious world citizens. We understand needing extra downtime or stimuli protection does not make us "delicate flowers"— merely human beings safeguarding our nervous systems. As we embrace our traits through growth and learning, we become more skillful self-advocates. Eventually, caring for ourselves becomes second nature.

Self-Care Strategies to Try

Need fresh self-care inspiration? Consider integrating these practices:

Morning routine - Start your day slowly with gentle movement, hydration, journaling, and breakfast. Avoid rushing into work chaos.

Digital boundaries - Set limits on news consumption and social media scrolling, which overtax HSPs. Unplug for blocks of time.

Nature immersion - Spend time outdoors daily, even if brief—a powerful antidote to modern stress.

Exercise - Maintain an exercise routine meeting your energy levels. Yoga and walking fortify us without draining us.

Comfort foods - Keep nutritious snacks on hand. Eat little meals often to stabilize blood sugar and moods.

Supplementary downtime - Take mini-breaks plus extra rest days. Give yourself permission to recharge often.

Meditation - Practice calming, centering meditation or breathwork to relieve overwhelm and anxiety.

As your self-care skills strengthen, you'll feel more energized and resilient in your daily life. With time, self-nurturing becomes second nature. Setbacks will happen, but don't be deterred. Growth is not linear. Learning your sensory needs and standing firmly in them transforms life for highly sensitive beings. You'll uncover your true power harnessed through self-care and mindfully crafted boundaries.

d. Cultivating Self-Confidence and Assertiveness

As highly sensitive beings, we often struggle with assertiveness and self-confidence. We may feel unsure about speaking up, stating our needs clearly, or pushing back against mistreatment. Our heightened empathy can make us excellent listeners and supporters of others yet poor advocates for our own well-being.

Luckily, assertiveness is a skill we can cultivate. As we better understand our sensitive natures, we can build confidence from within to communicate effectively while honoring our hearts.

Overcoming People-Pleasing Tendencies

Many HSPs are natural "people pleasers." We want close connections, so we may over-extend trying to make everyone happy. We ignore mounting resentment as our needs go unmet. Learning to set boundaries gracefully prevents burning out from endless caretaking. Start simply saying "no" to non-essentials, allowing you to serve your priorities better.

The view needs to be assertive, not aggressive. State them calmly, respectfully explaining your reasoning. Ask directly for accommodations to manage stimulation or stress at work, with friends, even loved ones. Compassion must begin with self. Healthy relationships only form once both parties feel seen.

Trust Your Emotional Radar

Highly sensitive people possess profound emotional intelligence and insight into subtle relationship dynamics. We pick up on tension or discomfort that goes unnoticed by others. Yet we frequently second-guess our inner wisdom, wondering if we are "overreacting." Recall times your sensitivity empowered you to elegantly resolve conflict or help others. You likely have excellent "people instincts"—learn to trust them.

See Sensitivity as an Asset

Through our nervous system's heightened awareness, we notice things that less sensitive individuals overlook. Our ability to deeply empathize allows us to connect profoundly. Although the noisy modern world overtaxes us, we are not inherently "flawed." Our sensitivity becomes a tremendous asset in environments and careers playing to our strengths. We simply require extra care customizing conditions to meet our needs. Define success on your own terms.

Embrace the Journey

Boosting confidence and assertiveness requires commitment as highly sensitive beings. But each small step compounds, gradually transforming how we advocate for our well-being. We unravel old assumptions about our "limits," moving through fear into new realms of self-acceptance. Each breakthrough leads to another until assertiveness feels natural. Soon, we show up fully expressed, grounded in our sensitivity, leading from the heart with gentle power.

As we conclude our exploration of managing sensitivity, I feel honored to have shared this journey with you. May you embrace your gifts, thrive in work and relationships, and change the world by boldly being your sensitive self. There is no other quite like you. Our next chapter explores seizing growth opportunities as highly intuitive lifelong learners.

Onward we go together!

CHAPTER 8

PERSONAL GROWTH AND LIFELONG LEARNING

Dear fellow travelers, our lengthy passage through the oceans of self-discovery now nears its closing shores. Hasn't this voyage proved more wondrous than any imagined? We sighted mystical terrains never glimpsed by companionless eyes, aided buoyantly by fellowship's swift currents.

Together, we've absorbed lifesaving navigational tools for reconciling a world often hostile towards uncommon souls. We conquered inner demons, reinvented limiting narratives, and ignited creative purpose once obscured in shadowy depths. Doesn't pride surge in our collective chests, recalling terrain overcome?

Yet while our sturdy vessel steers toward the destination's safe harbors, mighty swells still heave on the horizon. Our sailing course holds potential for both ecstasy and sorrow before the earth again greets foot soles. But we stand gallant, spirits tested through trials past. Wisdom gathered has seasoned reactive minds into discerning instruments precisely tuned to life's multi-textured cadences.

So brace together, crew, as tumultuous waters approach! Our captain commands full focus toward infinite possibility waiting beyond sorrow's veil. We've stored provisions for whatever unfolds by absorbing lessons from chapters past. Remember, sensitivity's very essence is fluidity and growth, should we allow it. Even impending grief propels evolution should we shift perspective.

I confess both giddy anticipation and melancholy stir already for me, realizing each sentence typed further us from shared exploration's beginning, closer toward inevitable parting. Yet what grand adventures await the application of hard-won tools gathered together? We are ready now to implement this program for living sensitivity boldly.

First then, before we disembark, important guidance remains regarding navigating change courageously. So, come; let's savor a few more treasured leagues joined in common cause. Our journey will not end until the shorelines fully materialize!

Now then, as we prepare to implement lessons gathered on taming life's changes graciously, let's address overcoming resistance practically by...

a. The continuous journey of personal growth for HSPs

Personal growth is an ongoing process that evolves as we deepen our self-understanding. By embracing curiosity, flexibility, and mindfulness, we can approach change courageously while unlocking our creative talents and leading deeply fulfilling lives.

Curiosity as a Driving Force for Personal Growth

Curiosity fuels the Highly Sensitive Person's quest for meaning and self-discovery. Our minds constantly ponder life's mysteries, seeking to comprehend humanity's purpose amidst the cosmos. We ask why suffering exists, how society might elevate consciousness, and what unseen forces move within our souls. This insatiable questioning propels our personal growth.

As knowledge-seekers, learning is oxygen for sensitive minds. We share philosopher's wonder in the face of uncharted frontiers ripe for exploration. The sensitive scholar analyzes poetry's nuances, just as the sensitive scientist marvels at quarks' quantum dance. Both reveal truth's prism, refracting understanding.

When curiosity guides us, stale paradigms topple. Outworn assumptions dissolve, yielding innovation. Growth depends not on gathering additional facts but on daring beliefs' destruction. Thus, curiosity's first step calls us beyond comfortable harbors into awe's adventures. Only by abandoning certainty's shores do we expand perspective and evolve spiritually.

The Sensitive's Adaptability: Navigating Life's Changes

While craving comprehension, HSPs still find certainty elusive. Unforeseen change ambushes our best-laid plans, forcing adaptation. Financial shifts, career detours, health crises, or lost relationships demand flexibility if we're to survive, much less thrive.

Might we frame life's upsets as opportunities? Flowing with change resembles rushing water carving stone. Resistance brings pain; acceptance shapes destiny. Each unexpected twist holds the potential for self-discovery should we release rigid expectations. Through practicing non-attachment to envisioned outcomes, we gain pliancy, poised to capitalize on unseen options revelation soon unveils.

When we cast aside useless baggage, traveling light quickens our pace. Adaptability means ransacking assumptions annually, retaining only robust truths that uplift and inspire. Our receptive minds crave continuous input, remaining open to modification should persuasive evidence arise.

Welcoming life's changes with relaxed expectations liberates sensitive people for creative responses. We surf each transition with poise when acknowledging impermanence and the futility of clutching certainty. Amidst the maelstrom, we spot guidance from an expanding vision not graspable before. Such growth sprouts from the seated presence, not strained striving.

Change as an Opportunity for Growth

While honoring the past, revelations arise by fixing sight ahead, not behind. Beyond familiar shores, unmapped waters entice our seeking vessels ever forward.

Though former selves once served us nobly, could we lovingly release their limiting beliefs as one sheds outworn garb? Might we travel unfettered by redundant assumptions that blink our perspective?

As sensitive beings, disillusionment and doubt cannot dim youth's lingering idealism within hopeful hearts. When obstacles arise, we intrinsically ask what lies beyond them. Curiosity whispers that each barrier unveiled lifts the veiling itself, promising epiphanies. Our faith rests in the possibility of transformation, though paths remain unclear.

By acknowledging outdated internal contracts are no longer binding, we free ourselves for destiny's full manifestation. History lies littered with starved visionaries clinging to models, never questioning until conversions came too late. Like fledglings sensing first flight, sensitive creatures thrive through inhabiting change's threshold that fortifies timid wings.

So dare lift eyes to horizons far surpassing present parameters and glimpse approaching wonders birthed by only the bravest, most quizzical minds, for yours may prove among sensitive legions destined to impact humanity's next unfolding.

Strategies for Approaching Change with a Sensitive Mindset

When facing impending changes as highly sensitive people, developing constructive mindsets and practices better equips us for navigating transitions with minimal chaos. By organizing reactions into healthy channels in advance, we prevent unwieldy overwhelm threatening sensitive systems. Let's explore beneficial strategies for facing change courageously.

Cultivate Non-Attachment

Clinging to desired outcomes often sabotages their achievement. Grasping originates from a primal fear of loss. Yet fiercely guarding imagined futures locks perception, blinding intuition's vision essential for recognizing unforeseen possibilities change soon unveils.

Through practicing mindful non-attachment, we release perceived security found by perpetually planning. When insisting on certainty, anxieties arise. But by adopting open-minded flexibility, we permit higher forces to organize optimal destinies on our behalf. From this posture of allowing, clarity unfolds, illuminating once-obscured pathways.

Thus, we progress not through vainly trying to control external variables but by focusing solely on the right inner response. When aligning actions with ethics and wisdom, desired manifestations naturally unfold.

Rewrite Assumptions

To best utilize change for growth, scrutinize assumptions requiring updating. We often ascribe excess power to childhood imprints without realizing evolutionary maturity brings necessary amendments into perspective.

For instance, direct environmental experiences provided limited outlooks; exploring broader inputs expands understanding. Our initial political views, relationship needs, or ethical positions may require adjustment upon exposure to additional truthful data or through awakening higher discernment.

By regularly re-evaluating internal paradigms against incoming evidence, we harness change for maximizing personal growth rather than reactively rejecting progress.

Preempt Discomforts

Change often spurs discomfort—an unavoidable aspect of growth. By mentally preparing for difficulties, we reduce the likelihood of being broadsided by challenges inevitably arising during transitional seasons.

For instance, when changing jobs, we can expect career adjustments requiring upskilling. Or purchasing first homes may entail unforeseen repairs. Starting meditation routines summons initial restlessness before the stabilized calm.

Thus, when facing impending change, honest appraisal of potential discomforts permits practical preparation, logical troubleshooting, and psychological readiness, allowing smooth navigation in spite of wrinkles. Facing fear clears its ability to freeze or disturb us.

Overcoming Fear and Resistance to Change

Despite potential growth change offers, alterations often provoke fear and resistance. By understanding the psychological drivers of such reactions, HSPs can intentionally shift counterproductive stances, slowing positive progress. Let's examine why we reflexively oppose change and how to transcend barriers.

Identify Core Fears

When change looms, pause and investigate arising emotions. Sensations of nervousness or foreboding frequently indicate fear's presence. Pinpoint what scenario you truly dread and why this outcome inspires concern.

For example, starting therapy may surface anxiety that painful topics will emerge, leaving you depressed. Or changing jobs could represent financial fears and lost security if things don't work out. Openly acknowledging precise worries is essential for strategizing solutions.

Challenge Catastrophic Thinking

Once you uncover specific change-related fears, candidly question if your concerns are fully realistic. Highly sensitive people often catastrophize, envisioning worst-case fallouts which seldom materialize. This mental habit harms by obscuring balanced thinking required for clear-eyed decision-making.

Invite grounded companions (or therapists) to helpfully challenge fear-based assumptions regarding change outcomes. Perhaps you are ignoring obvious SOC (strengths, opportunities, or contingencies) you could leverage to prevent imagined disaster? What fresh potential arises if envisioning success?

Rewrite Familiar Stories

Resistance also flows from narrating change through frameworks of past difficulties—"I tried school before and couldn't handle it" or "A previous job transition went terribly." This mental groove likely formed in childhood when pivotal moves provoked lasting injury.

But the past cannot dictate today's experience if desired outcomes are consciously asserted. Your life transforms when consciously rewriting personal narratives. Affirm, "I welcome beneficial change nourishing my growth." Thus, inner soil improves, allowing roots to blossom in any environment through intentionally planting empowering beliefs.

And so we arrive at our present frontier, contemplating the next steps forward while integrating lessons learned. By embracing uncertainty as an ally, not an adversary, highly sensitive people unlock our vast potential. For once, sensing unguarded possibility winking beyond fear's silhouettes, we feel destiny's full call. Shall we continue walking this path together? Abundant terrain awaits further charting...

b. The importance of curiosity, learning, and adaptation

Sensitivity and creativity share an innate bond—heightened perception unleashes vision. Yet without resilience and adaptively nurturing our receptive spirits amid inevitable overwhelms, creative flames risk being extinguished by storms before fully illuminating. This section specifically explores how learning and curiosity-fueled growth allow our sensitive gifts to flourish, transforming each challenge into fuel-empowering purpose.

Let's ignite inspiration together!

The Link Between Sensitivity and Creativity

My friends know when I'm hit with a creative spark because my eyes grow wide with excitement. Ideas flood my imagination in vivid technicolor as I grab my journal, quickly scribbling words and sketches to capture the inspiration surging wildly. Lost in creative flow, I'm oblivious to the passing hours. Emerging finally, blinking with surprise that darkness crept in, my sensitive spirit feels wonderfully tapped.

This innate link between heightened sensitivity and artistic expression intrigues me deeply. We Highly Sensitive People soak in subtle life textures missed by others, moved profoundly by poignancy often overlooked. My theory is such acute aesthetic attunement naturally spills into creative longings, giving form to elusive beauty sensed under life's surface. I ache to translate ineffable emotions into metaphors and symbols you understand through my words and images. Its intensity transcended into art.

Visionaries throughout history certainly displayed sensitivity's creative hallmarks. Consider brilliant innovators like Steve Jobs, Alan Turing, or Ada Lovelace, who revolutionized technology by manifesting remarkable inner visions outwardly. Artistic masters including Virginia Woolf, Claude Monet, and Beethoven produced era-defining works channeling exquisite sensitivities into lasting cultural treasures. Leaders across spheres—Gloria Steinem, Abraham Lincoln, Martin Luther King—wielded sensitive pens passionately, reforming policies that oppressed marginalized groups. Often, what outsiders label "weakness" in such pioneers, they reframed as strength fueling world-changing creative purpose.

So next artists block strikes, recall your sensitive nervous system's specialized design attunes you to the nuanced aesthetic richness, filling creative wells. What initially overwhelms contains seed potential, birthing your most visionary expressions. You inhabit a gorgeous world awaiting your unique translations. Now skillfully channel the glorious sensitive you - and let inspiration flow unfiltered through your instrument out into the wider world awaiting your gifts. Our perspectives deserve to manifest creatively.

The Continuous Journey of Personal Growth for Highly Sensitive People

Fellow sensitive being, can you believe how much we've grown together already? What once seemed just my lonely burden now connects us as a community embracing sensitivity's challenges and gifts. We've mapped common storms weathered and tools nurturing calm within them. Life's colors shine brighter now, and intricacies are noticed with compassion, not judgment. Still ahead, new horizons await charting. I cannot wait to discover with you!

But pause first, appreciating the distance overcome. We began believing something was wrong within our tender skins and hearts. Society's blunt tools lacked precision, nurturing delicate essence. Yet now we know nervous systems tuned acutely developmentally vary, not defectively so. Science explains our perceptive antennae insightfully scan depths most miss. With this knowledge, we rewrite stories of lack and embrace sensitivity's strengths compassionately.

And when storms still arrive, we take heart, remembering they pass—resilience fortified by choosing self-care, not self-attack. We float now, buoyed by hard-won self-knowledge protecting boundaries and balancing stimulate-rest rhythms preventing overwhelm's capsize. The world may spin fiercely, but inner stillness grounds perspective clear and undistorted by churning emotions. We inhabit sensitivity's fullness at last.

I wonder what creative solutions your distinctive experiences will uncover to improve life for fellow Highly Sensitive People? How will mentoring others unleash their gifts too? My intuition is that your expanded empathy and understanding of this human variance will powerfully spawn new inclusive environments if you dare to dream and then act boldly. But first, more awaits uncovering on our shared personal growth voyage.

c.   Exercises and techniques to tap into creative potential as an HSP

Fellow sensitive soul, let's explore how we can nurture our innate creative talents! As deeply perceptive beings, we possess a natural reservoir of imagination, inspiration, and vision. Yet, often in youth, standardized education, and social norms condition us to conform, dimming creative expression. Now, as adults, we may wonder if it's too late to unlock creative gifts long buried under responsibility's weight.

I assure you, it's never too late! Our distinctive minds thrive when crafting, innovating, and self-expressing. We feel most vibrant, creating worlds where our emotional spectrum fits. Through gentle encouragement coaxing long dormant talents now, confidence builds, manifesting precious visions outward. So, shall we begin awakening creative potential awaiting awareness? I'll share my journey igniting creative courage.

Honoring Childlike Curiosity's Return

As a child, my imagination overflowed, crafting elaborate fictional realms where I adventured as a protagonist. My bedroom sanctuary harbored landscapes, and characters sprung fully formed from some mysterious wellspring. I fashioned villages populating dolls' fantasy lives for hours. Such immersive world-building occupied endless freedom found in youth.

Yet adolescence's self-conscious arrival soon dismissed "childish flights of fancy" as immaturity. Impressing peers suddenly mattered more than creative exploration. Over the years, I incrementally relinquished magical inner sanctums for social survival until one morning I awoke, finding imagination atrophied, that once abundant creative stream now arid wasteland. Conformity had erased identity's core.

It took counseling first, gingerly excavating the barren terrain holding fading embers of talent taken for granted. My therapist challenged me, simply noticing each creative urge without judgment as it sparked. "Perhaps external achievement matters less than mindfully creating just for the process. Start small simply reconnecting, then build as interest flows," she suggested. "Growth unfolds organically when we stop forcing outcomes."

Her wisdom freed gently, nurturing creativity without demanding perfection or commodifiable results. I began casually journaling, then painting leisurely again until riots of color canvassed my walls. Soon, long abandoned passions crescendoed into starting this book, likewise reawakening my slumbering gifts. Try rediscovering youthful creative joy too!

Strategies for Unlocking Natural Gifts in Adulthood

We late bloomers require compassion, patience, and perseverance to reclaim creativity suppressed by necessity and expectations. Begin practicing self-love because shame sabotages expressions' flow state. There exists no "right way" to create, so cease seeking validation from perceived authority figures. Instead, set intentions to honor your distinctive needs and talents.

Start small, incorporating creativity into daily moments. Doodle during tedious conferences, infuse favorite hobbies with artistic embellishment and engage all senses by preparing comforting meals. Let inspiration guide your hours, not a rigid agenda. Make space for play, adventure, and novelty beyond productivity. Schedule regular self-dates spent in any way rejuvenating spirit.

Permission granted to go at your pace fully nurtures growth. Some days allow simply appreciating others' talents. Creativity manifests uniquely through every distinct nervous system. Comparing achievements often breeds envy and self-sabotage rather than motivation. Instead, define personal metrics for satisfaction to minimize criticism hijacking enjoyment. Focus on process, not perfection.

Develop a beginner's mind by observing the world curiously—approach learning as a lifelong endeavor, not a burden. Mimic children's shameless engagement is driven solely by delight. Infuse even mundane tasks with openness to beauty hiding in plain sight. Soon, fresh eyes discern inspiration everywhere.

What if creativity itself became a goal, not a means towards external ends? View creating akin to moving body through a beloved dance. The experience itself adorns existence's routines capes with poetry facilitating flow states. Mindfulness lets us inhabit the creative process fully rather than rushing towards some finished product.

So, reawaken the inner child eagerly scribbling wild imaginative stories with crayons. No deadline hovers, no expectations demand scalable outcomes. Remember before achievement-driven mentality conditioned creativity's constraint? Revisit by intentionally carving space beyond responsibility. Play, create, meander aimlessly once again.

Who knows what dormant talents and passions resurface through unstructured space, reconnecting senses and inspiring expression? Allow ideas percolating since adolescence now transform scribbles into literary legacy or ballet dreams into community studio nurturing movement's creative release. My prayer is reclaiming your distinctive creative birthright, untethered wings awaiting flight towards destiny.

We each view the world uniquely through distinctive, sensitive lenses. What glimmers may emerge, magnifying individual essence when cradling creativity gently once more? Perhaps our shared continued journey unveils the truth together.

d. Guidance on embracing change and challenges with a sensitive mindset

Whether minor or major, change often proves challenging for us highly sensitive people. Our deeply feeling natures crave stability and continuity, so shifts in routines or environments easily unsettle our equilibrium. Sudden announcements about impending transitions at work or home may stir anxiety even if ultimately beneficial. We require extra time to mentally prepare for new chapters unfolding.

Yet avoiding or resisting change is rarely constructive in the long term. Through intentionally cultivating acceptance, flexibility, and trust, we sensitive beings build resilience by navigating life's flowing river. My prayer is the following guidance on consciously embracing change with compassion aids all fellow sojourners. Read slowly, integrating insights as they resonate. Our shared path toward wholeness awaits!

Cultivating Acceptance of Change

Might we adopt a gentle beginner's mind, observing life's unfolding with curiosity, not fear? Rather than tightly grasping control of what lies ahead, we create space for optimal outcomes, already organizing on our behalf.

Could releasing rigid expectations about envisioned futures ease the worry of something going "wrong"? By practicing mindful presence, we disempower obsolete mental scripts based on past trials that still echoing. This moment alone holds power, determining our peace.

What if embracing reality as IS freed us to appreciate exactly this now? Fretting cannot hasten destiny's flow or control scenes fate directs. We are mere players following cosmic cues revealed step by step. Exhaling, we walk on lighthearted, come what may.

Discovering Opportunity Amidst Transition

Rather than viewing shifts through the lens of loss or threat, what new possibilities appear, focusing ahead with optimism? Beyond reassurances of "this too shall pass," how might fresh trajectories enrich if welcoming the unknown's wisdom with an adventurous spirit?

Might we lean curiously into change, inquiring what unique growth or strengths its challenges could unveil in the season ahead? Flow resembles a mighty river carving rough stones into smooth sands. By riding rapids with faith, we emerge gently polished, flowing harmoniously onwards.

What dreams or callings surface when changing tides redirect? Perhaps upended security blankets, though discomfiting initially, free us finally manifesting formerly ignored talents. Necessity breeds invention; limitations prompt resourcefulness. By embracing uncertainty courageously, we discover providence working through every redirection. Onwards in trust!

Adapting Sensitively to Daily Demands

Navigating modernity's lightning pace and endless input strains sensitive systems built for gentler eras. Challenges stacking exponentially quicken heart rates already bounding. How carefully can we preserve equilibrium amidst such velocity and volume?

As highly attuned instruments, what modifications must we implement to such environments to nurture, not negate our gifts? Communicating needs for sanctuary's restorative silence seems non-negotiable, as do consistent self-care practices fortifying resilience. By wisely stabilizing foundations, daily demands feel surmountable through balanced planning and proactive damage control.

Rather than resenting obligations depleting limited energy reserves, consciously monitoring stimulation levels prevents hitting emotional breaking points. Gently request assistance when near capacity; saying "no" to additional tasks models healthy boundaries benefitting all. Then, creatively infuse menial moments with artistry, discovering beauty amidst monotony. Our sensitive selves thrive when honoring natural flows. Through focus and flow, we masterfully conduct life's quickening cadence.

In conclusion, my friends, our shared expedition through sensitivity's labyrinths now concludes, yet actually only just begun! For living this human journey awakens daily invitations, growing into our deepest wholeness. Many insights gathered here nurture that continual blooming wherever roads meander next. You've awakened, so arise courageously, sensitively shining ever brighter blessing circles small and grand through your distinctive palette of perceptual gifts. The world awaits your creative revolution!

I treasured walking these miles together. Perhaps our paths will cross again some glorious day once this book manifests fully. For now, farewell, dear hearts!

Go gracefully, boldly, exquisitely YOU. You are the change this evolving world most needs...

CONCLUSION

We've now reached the closing pages of our shared journey exploring the maze of life as highly sensitive people. When we first set out together, sensitivity felt like an overwhelming tide constantly threatening to pull us under—stirring anxiety instead of calm, distance instead of connection. Its mirror reflected shame staring back, a damning list of flaws crying out for correction. Our gifts faded into deficits in the piercing light of this false narrative. Our superpowers are muted by a world shouting that sensitive souls must toughen up or face exclusion.

But as we traveled deeper into self-understanding alongside fellow sojourners, revelation dawned. We realized high sensitivity indicates not brokenness but specialized neurobiology and genetics built for distinct purposes. As researchers uncovered measurable nervous system and biological differences, suddenly, our emotions and acute awareness made sense as intended design, not disorder. We learned that temperaments landing on this subjective spectrum of sensing bring evolutionary strengths like enhanced threat detection, cautious decision-making, rich, intuitive wisdom, and a profound capacity for healing and empathy.

Armed with this paradigm shift in perspective, we set about writing a new story starring sensory superheroes, not damaged sidekicks. We mapped common challenges arising from the heightening of life's beauties and burdens alike. Frequently overwhelmed and easily exhausted, we created daily sanctuaries for stillness to settle spinning minds. Wrestling fear of judgment, we practiced radical self-acceptance. Through understanding sensory processing sensitivity as an innate filter for perceiving what others often overlook, we transformed persistence into empowered purpose. Relationships rippled with awakened authenticity as we discovered voice courageously speaking long-suppressed emotion. No more severing expression to fit narrow molds that were never meant for blooming orchids like us anyhow!

Standing firmly rooted in self-knowledge today, we bear storms and soak in inspiration equally while riding balancing waves skillfully between. We now recognize high sensitivity's wellspring nourishing our most soulful callings—writing, healing, creating, advocating, and more, for vision emerges through eyes attuned, noticing scarce resources and reimagining realms free from injustice—sensitivity seeds transformation by compelling crusaders to question the status quo. Our receptive nervous systems absorb the suffering most turn from until it spills back out as courage and conscience-guided action.

Three Key Takeaways for Thriving:

1. Shift Perspective on Sensitivity

The most pivotal first step on the path towards embracing our sensitive nature involves fundamentally reframing how we perceive our trait's purpose and value. Do we continue viewing heightened emotional and sensory processing as abnormal liability stealing peace? Or do we trust science revealing this as a specialized design priming us for empathy, insight, and visionary guidance? This conscious choice in perspective lays the foundations determining destiny's direction. From acceptance blooms motivation, nurturing sensitivity instead of attacking it.

2. Cultivate Customized Self-Care

Thriving while highly sensitive requires consistently caring compassionately for our uncommon needs. Due to extra receptivity and responsiveness, we tend to deplete limited energy faster than others if not replenishing adequately. Constructing daily rituals and spaces mitigating overstimulation prevents emotional extremes taxing relationships and productivity. We flourish by honoring natural introverted and contemplative rhythms through boundaries around stimulation. Maximizing sensitive strengths means minimizing triggers through customized self-nurturance.

3. Communicate Your Experience

The final key for sensitive people managing challenges while maintaining rich perceptual gifts is transparently conveying our experience to loved ones. Without a proper understanding of heightened sensitivity, our reactions appear unreasonable through mainstream lenses. Educate those close to you—verbalize the need for flexibility at work, quiet spaces to recharge energy, and extra processing time before responding. Frame sensitivity as a specialized trait, not personal weakness or attempt manipulation. From comprehension blooms tolerance supporting you being beautifully you.

By embracing this empowering, sensitive-positive perspective and then consistently caring for our uncommon requirements with compassion, we transpire from drained to thriving. Our gifts pour out, no longer trapped behind floodgates blocking external criticism or judgment. We walk as integrated, sensitive beings fully embodied, fulfilled, and seen.

Now, What Lies Ahead? Nurturing & Sharing Your Gifts Dear fellow sensitive soul, can you believe how far we've come already? I don't know about you, but after learning so much about my traits through our shared journey, I feel as though I'm inhabiting a whole new reality! I used to tiptoe through life, feeling constantly bombarded and seeking invisibility, so my "overreactions" went unnoticed. Now, though, while still carefully managing my energy, I move through each day with confidence rooted in self-knowledge. Understanding my hardwired sensitivity helps me communicate needs effectively across all environments. Instead of hiding my tearful sentimentality, I let it inspire my writing and photography. I educated close friends about my introversion, requiring ample downtime between social gatherings, so they no longer feel hurt if I politely decline after-work happy hours when they are depleted. My whole existence flows smoother now that I'm gently aligned with my authentic rhythms and inner compass.

Our voyage together cultivated so much fruitful self-awareness. We peeled off layers of assumptions and criticism obscuring the exquisite essence within. We dared to love ourselves fully - sensory intensity, asynchronous rhythms, tearfulness, and all! I wonder now, looking outward (as we HSPs tend to do), what dreams might you bravely step into on the horizon? How will nurturing sensitivity's creative depths manifest?

Might I gently challenge us both to lean further into purpose awakened on this journey? Whispers arising from your resonant emotional world signal scores awaiting orchestration through myriad mediums—poetry, advocacy, leadership, community development, counseling, nature conservation, and so much more. We sensitive beings entered this earth plane to infuse environments with the very beauty, meaning, and hope realized internally once we transformed self-judgment into self-care. It's time now to courageously embody our soulful callings outwardly.

I implore you, what injustice or scarcity in this hurting world elicits your tears until they spill into heroic involvement and solution-making? What unique emotional wisdom sensed subtly, will you voice on behalf of the muted? My dear one, your compassion compels speaking poetry to be perceived alone presently. Your gifts long to uplift humanity's higher liberation. All creation awaits your blessing.

Our last shared milestone involves amalgamating insights gathered so you may carry these inner torches forward as beacons on the path ahead. My prayer is contemplating these questions ignites courage summoning destiny:

~ What specifically resonated most deeply from our collective discussions? Circle key ideas or experiences uncovered.

~ How have your perspectives shifted through absorbing fellow sojourners' stories and struggles? What limiting self-judgments transformed into self-compassion?

~ Which personal or professional breakthroughs have emerged already since implementing sensitivity-informed communication or self-care?

~ Looking inward then outward, where might your emotional attunement, empathy, and passions most empower improvement around you?

I cannot wait to hear accounts of you thriving while boldly bringing sensitivity's guidance into all spheres - home, work, community, and our world at large! As transformational leaders, HSPs naturally excel in facilitating renewal by first modeling the change we wish to see. So now, let your hard-won light shine brightly, blessing circles small and grand through your distinctive perceptual palette. The future beckons your creative revolution!

No matter what awaits around the river bend, I'm honored to have walked this winding passage with you. Our bonding through shared vulnerability watered seeds of wisdom, sprouting fresh direction and purpose. Whenever you need encouragement remembering the beauty of your uncommon journey, return here, retracing insights gathered as beloved companions, for sensitivity's flow gifts us with extremely personal yet universally resonant experiences once embraced fully.

Thank you for your authentic presence on this journey... Now, spread your wings—the sky awaits!

In closing, I affirm love and blessings into your unfolding, fellow wayfinder. May you inhabit each day with renewed perspective, nurturing sensitivity as the superpower it is. When storms inevitably come billowing in from all directions, as happens when exploring uncharted inner territory, recall tools gathered in our protected cove. The light ahead always proves mightier, revealing safe passage even when temporarily obscured from limited sight.

Together, we walk on with courage, dismantling inner and outer barriers constraining our wholeness and liberating wider circles too through humility's quiet activism. We dwell in an empowered community aligned to raise the frequency vibrating out from healed hearts. All the world awaits this healing conduction, so lead the conduction!

Through every season, sensitivity's ebb and flow carries you into existence's glorious depths, then tenderly back out again when your breath runs short. This current never overwhelms faithfully guided ones, knowing secrets swimming skillfully alongside life's essential essence within. So splash freely here with exuberant trust; the waters are your beloved home.

Let's swim on as one, gazing back occasionally and ahead often, fully engaged, honoring today's mysterious invitations into existence. Our whole adventure continues, fellow catalyzers emboldened now carrying codes for humanity's evolution compassionately cracked open through the wisdom of sensitive souls!

Your Opinion Matters

Loved the journey through my book?

Your thoughts matter! Share your review and help others discover the magic.

Scan the QR code or Click here to leave your feedback. Let the world know what you think!

Scan here!

Printed in Great Britain
by Amazon

46729066R00073